# A Game Ball for Frank

A Journey of Respect, Gratitude, and Redemption

by
Jamie King

# A Game Ball for Frank

A Journey of Respect, Gratitude, and Redemption

by
Jamie King

All photos credit:Mark A. Rolland Photography

ISBN: 978-1540700681
Library of Congress Control Number: 2016919864

Published by Kokorozashi Press
Fredericksburg, VA

For more information, visit: AGameBallForFrank.com
Or contact info@AGameBallForFrank.com

# Table of Contents

## Part 4 – Family and the Future 115

## Addressing the Issue of Abuse 133

# Game Balls (Acknowledgements)

**Mom**, I know you are on high watching over us and your presence is felt every day. I love you more than words could ever say, and I thank you again for always having my back and for fighting for me and with me when I needed it the most. You are the best mom a son could ever hope to have for instilling the beliefs in me and my brothers that we could do anything if we went after it and believed we could.

**Denise**, Thank you for always believing in me, for being such a big part of my success, and for making sure everything ran so smoothly behind the scenes with the football team, enabling me to focus on the on field aspects. I love you so much, and you have made me so happy and given me such an amazing sense of family. I have always felt that you believed I was capable of doing great things, and you have been such a stabilizing force and someone that helped me put the pieces back together for which I will always be grateful.

**Jennie**, I am proud of your outstanding academic achievements at Virginia Tech. I am proud of the daughter you have always been, as well as the mother of our beautiful grandchildren. Your work ethic is amazing, and you do a great job of balancing work and home life. I want you to know that there are great things ahead for you. I know your career path has some exciting things ahead!

**Patrick**, I am proud of your record-setting athletic career and your full ride to Illinois as one of the top kickers in the nation in 2000. I am also very proud of you for entering the Navy and working to protect our nation as a member aboard the USS Lincoln. Continue to pursue excellence in all you do and there is nothing you can't do!

**Ryan, Jillian, & Nathan**, I could not be prouder of the three of you, and I have always done my very best for each of you. I have talked to all three of you about being grateful for people in your life who have shown you kindness. I am proud that you are all respectful, and that you all have parents and grandparents that love you more than words can say. I will tell you what I always told your mother and Uncle Patrick: Be A Leader, Never Be A Follower and Do It Because It's Right Not Because Its Popular. I love you all and I am so very proud to be your Grampy!

**Steve, Earl, Brett, and Kelly**, The best brothers anyone could ever wish for. We may all have chosen different paths but never forget that Mom's biggest hope was that the one path we would always take would be the one back to each other because she wanted to make sure that we always stayed together. I love you all and I'm very proud of all that each of you have accomplished!

**Mark Moseley**, Thank you for doing something that had never been done before by an athlete of your stature, and for forever changing the lives of the young men and everyone associated with the Fredericksburg Generals. Thank you personally for believing in me and for leading us to a National Championship.

**Mark Rypien**, Thank you for taking a chance on a young kid with a dream, and for letting me be a part of the biggest moments of your athletic career! I will always be grateful to you and for our friendship.

**Mark Ryhanych**, What a long way we have come – from a brawl for it all at Stafford Middle School to a lifelong friendship, to a record-setting offense and a National Championship. It would not have happened without you, and I thank you for making the Generals passing game as lethal as it was. You are the best quarterback that has ever played Minor League Football, and it was so special to have done it together.

**Steve Carey**, There is no one that has been there more or longer, and who knows me better and vice versa. You have always been a leader in the community as a top police officer in Stafford County. You have been a loving husband to your one-of-a-kind wife, Cheryl, and your beautiful daughters, Kendall and Kelsey. I have known you since we were in elementary school, and we have been close ever since. There is nothing I would not do for you, and my life has been enriched beyond words to have had you in it. Thank you for setting the bar so high and for showing me in your daily walk that anything is possible. You also helped me through my darkest, toughest days, and I will always be grateful to you for being there when I needed you the most! I love you!

**Kevin Brown**, Thank you for your friendship for the last 30-plus years. You are the best high school basketball coach there is, and you are a friend that has made me a better person just for knowing you! Thank you for allowing me to coach with you and help your teams. There is no one that is brighter than you, no one that coaches like you. You are one of the greatest college players that ever played, and you have surpassed that as a coach, husband, father, and friend. I will always be thankful for your friendship. All the best to you and your wonderful wife Michelle. Casey, Lucas, and Autumn: I love you all.

**Mike Neville**, My broadcasting partner the man who started me on my career in broadcasting. You are a legend in the local community, and I have always felt that the local community has a treasure in you. I know you could be anywhere in the country doing radio or TV because you are so great at your craft. There is no one better than you when it comes to the radio. Your signature voice is something others only wish they could have. I can never thank you enough for giving a young broadcaster the opportunity to have some air time and grow as much as possible. You are more than a broadcaster to me; you have been a lifelong friend who has always been there for me, and that has always been appreciated. You are the best and I hope that one day soon your Bills win Super Bowl and that you receive a network job, because there is no one more deserving than you. I love you and thank you for making such a huge difference in my life. My very best to you, your wonderful wife Sharon, and your kids: Amber, Ian, Meghan, and Courtney.

This book would not have been possible without the work behind the scenes from **Tom Dozier**, Senior Editor for **RVA Gamebreak**. Thank you for all of your help and insight; you were amazing. I value your friendship and your advice, and I appreciate all of your efforts.

**Bethany Bradsher** is an amazing woman and a tremendous author who helped me get the book moving forward. I appreciate all that you did and thank you for your advice and all of your help and best of luck in the future with all of your books.

The guys at **Big Cloud Media, Paul and Dwayne Baptist**, were beyond great as they helped me get things shaped up and added certain aspects that I was too close to see were needed. I greatly appreciate them both. I appreciate you guys helping with the timeline and addressing all of the needs to help me have the best book possible. If you have any marketing or graphic needs go to www.bigcloudmedia.com/story they do it all, and they are super-talented, and I can't thank them enough for helping me get to the finish line.

The voiceover legend **Don LaFontaine**, who wanted to see *A Game Ball For Frank* become a movie: You provided the voice over for every major blockbuster movie that was ever made, thank you for your support in thinking my story could be very successful and well-received. Thank you for all that you did, and if it's meant to be it will be. The trailer that you did for my story was – in a word – amazing, and I can't thank you enough for all that you did.

*The Rookie*, **Jim Morris**, Thank you for helping me, and for all of the advice and guidance you offered. I loved your inspirational movie

*The Rookie*. You are a first-class person, and I wish you nothing but success and great health going forward. Your story is one that is amazing on every level, and your story continues to impact people every day. You are a sought-after speaker with an incredible message that everyone should hear.

*Mr. Invincible*, **Vince Papale**, thank you and Janet, your amazing wife, for your friendship, advice, and for giving me the positive feedback on my story! I loved your movie *Invincible* and you gave me great inspiration that I will be forever grateful for. Your charisma and drive are easy to see, and you achieved something many people thought was impossible. Thank you for showing people that if you have a dream you can realize it, if you do the things necessary to reach the goals you have set for yourself. You are an amazing speaker, and your story is one everyone should hear and see.

**Mike Singletary**, The greatest middle linebacker of them all. Thank you for your advice, friendship, and for inviting me to be a part of your coaching staff when you get your next opportunity. I believe in you, and I respect you. I know for a fact that you have a great plan in place for the next opportunity that you receive, and there is no doubt that you will be a major success when given the chance. There is no one better prepared than you. Your next opportunity is right around the corner, and I know when it comes you will make the most of it!

**Andre Collins**, Thank you for your friendship, and for showing me what a real Penn Stater is all about. You do an amazing job for the NFLPA, and your family (with 19 successful brothers and sisters who all went to college) is – in a word – amazing. You were a great Redskin, and one of the finest people I have ever known.

**Steve "Red" Tokarcik**, Thank you for your loyal friendship and for always being there for me. You helped mold me into the competitor I am, and you taught me great things about drive and never backing down no matter the opposition. We have been friends for over 30 years, and every time we get together it's like we picked up right where we left off. I love you, and thank you for always being the definition of a friend.

**Mark and Sandy Liotto and Family,** To our Florida family, thank you for your friendship and for always making us feel at home we look forward to seeing you soon and we always enjoy our time with you in sunny Florida!

**Mike LaCasse,** thank you for all of your help, for your long-time friendship, and for our fun times on the links! I look forward to many more. Always remember that no matter how things go for us we can always head out and play golf, so we have that going for us – which is nice!

**Ken Paradiso,** My main man Kenny P thank you for all you have done for me and for supporting me through the years. I am looking forward to great things from the ParaKings Company as the sky is the limit.

**Darrell Miller,** Thank you and your team at Fox Rothschild for all of your help and guidance with the story and for believing in me and for all of your help! You are amazing at what you do!

To the **Mountain View Wildcats** basketball players that I had a chance to work with: I hope you all continue on the path of success that started under **Coach Brown, Coach Pollock, Coach Maghan and Coach Darryl Mosley,** one of the finest groups of men and leaders I have ever known. Darryl Mosley is also widely known as a great pastor in our community at Stafford Crossings Community Church in Stafford, Virginia.

**Buck Albritton & Mitchell Bradley** and my friends at **ESPN 950AM,** Thank you for being great bosses, and for allowing me to have my own show on ESPN. It has been great working with you, and I thank you both for this unbelievable opportunity. I want to thank the great producers I have that have worked on my show: my main man **Andrew "Awall" Wallace, "Mid Major" Matt Josephs, and Denis Boateng,** who have helped make my show *The Sports*

*King* so special to be a part of. A special thanks to **Mitchell Bradley** who I met as a young energetic teenager and who years later gave me the opportunity to work with him based on my abilities, but also on the way that I treated him when he was a young man. Once again, it's a great lesson to always treat people with kindness and respect because you never know.

**Generals Coaches,** There is no National Championship without your blood, sweat, and continual efforts to make our football team great. We had the right mix of coaches that were not only great coaches but even better leaders of men. I am indebted to you all, and its because of you that we are National Champions! You were a class group of men that made each practice and game special to be a part of, and I thank you all for everything you did!

**Generals Players**, There is no magic without you; there is no success without you; there is no National Championship without you. You guys made a lifetime mission possible and in so doing you gave me one of the greatest career accomplishments of my life and for that I will always be grateful. There was no one better than you and you are deserving of being called the best Minor League Team Ever!

**Generals Support Staff,** we could not have done it without you and the efforts that you gave each week. Thank you for making things run so smoothly and for giving the fans a great game night experience. We want to thank our team Chiropractors **Dr. Jay Meggison** who worked with us and really added a much needed service in year one doing such a great job. **Dr. Gary Schulz** did an amazing job during the National Championship Season, and was essential to our team winning. We also want to thank our team Dentist **Dr. Adam K. Wyatt**.

**Generals Fans**, also known as the **Generals Army**, You were amazing game in and game out you filled up Maury Stadium and made Saturday night more than just a football game – it was an event! I can't thank you enough for making our home field advantage one-of-a-kind. We never lost a home game at Maury Stadium in the history of the Generals, and it was in large part due to you! Thank you. We all appreciated your support as you were undoubtedly the best fans in Minor League Football!

**Mike Wise,** The outstanding sports writer formerly of the Washington Post and currently with **ESPN's** *Undefeated.* Mike wrote the original story that was featured in the Washington Post Magazine, and he deserves a lot of credit for the outstanding feature he did on us. I appreciate his friendship, his help, and all that he has done. He is an amazing writer, and I wish the very best to him his wonderful wife Christina and his two boys.

**To all extended family, friends, coaches, teachers and anyone who ever believed in me,** Thank you because no one can do it alone. There are times along the journey when you may feel alone, but if I've said it once, I've said it a million times: We live in the greatest country on planet Earth, and there are so many wonderful, caring people that want to stop the cycle of abuse. My ultimate hope and prayer is that one day it will be eradicated once and for all!

**David & Helen Wolfe,** and their two outstanding daughters **Jemma and Sophie**: It is a rare person that can change the world, but **Leesa Mattress** CEO David Wolfe and his amazing team are doing just that. I can't put into words what David's friendship and mentoring have meant to me personally. He and his wife and daughters are first-class people who have always put others ahead of themselves. I am proud to be a friend of the Wolfes, and I want to thank David personally for all he has done for me, being such an integral part of my radio show both from a sponsorship standpoint and from content standpoint as well. Thank you for teaching me about Premier League Soccer, and for expanding my knowledge of a sport that is extremely exciting to watch. There is no doubt that Leesa will one day soon be the top selling mattress in the world because you do so much more than provide the best night's sleep ever: you change lives for the better through  your daily efforts and your 1-10 program, and that is something you should all be very proud of! Your parents and grandparents laid the foundation for your success when they told you that "giving back" is not an obligation – it's a privilege. You honor them every day with the outstanding give back program that is such a major part of what Leesa Mattress does to help people in need every day.

**Sonny Anderson**, A special thank you to the best equipment guy on Earth: Sonny Anderson from the **University of Michigan**. Congratulations on your wedding to your lovely wife Paige. You are a great dad to your son, Walter! Thank you and your outstanding staff for listening to *The Sports King* while at work at the University of Michigan. Good luck always, and Go Blue!

**Brian Smelter**, Special thanks to a great friend and a super talented person who knows audio/visual equipment and anything digital or computer-related like the back of his hand. Brian does amazing work at his business, **Flicko's,** where he does things with videos that are – in a word – incredible. He is a loyal friend who loves soccer beyond words – especially Barcelona, his favorite team. He has a wonderful family with wife Beth, his children, Ian and Kim.

**Andrew Fischer**, Thank you for all of your support and help with graphic design and artwork through the years. You are one of the most talented, innovative tech guys I've ever met. There is nothing you can't do in regards to a computer. I wish you the best with your movie, and hope it makes it to the big screen soon. Congratulations to you and your lovely wife Bethany on the birth of your son Jason James Fischer. I wish you continued success in all you do. You will do something great in the future, of that I have no doubt.

**Hal & Mary Lockhart**, Thank you for your friendship and advice through the years. Hal, you were a great competitor whose Richmond Ravens team was always ready. You always brought out the best in us. Congratulations on an amazing coaching career. You and Mary will not be judged on wins and losses, but by the countless lives you have affected over the 25 years as Coach and Owner of the

Richmond Ravens. Mary, you did an amazing job keeping the Mason-Dixon League and all of its coaches and administrators on the same page and you worked tirelessly to make the league something that we were all so very proud of. Thank you both for all you did to promote the game of football, and for being leaders in Richmond, Virginia for what you did both on and off the field.

**Kelly Hanna**, A special thank you to you and your outstanding marketing team at **Field Of Play Marketing**. I look forward to working with you and your great team and thank you for all you are doing for the story *A Game Ball for Frank*.

# Foreword by 1982 NFL MVP Mark Moseley

When asked by Jamie to write a foreword for his book on the semi-pro football team, the Generals, I thought, "If Jamie is able to capture the excitement, the enthusiasm, the dedication as well as the LOVE of football that these young men displayed at a time in their lives when they thought they were done playing the game, it will have been worth my time." Jamie is a good friend.

For me, it was the start of a new chapter in my life called "Life after Football". I had played in the NFL for 16 seasons. I had played in two Super Bowls. I had won almost every award as an NFL kicker that could be won. In 1982 I became the only kicker ever to win the NFL MVP Award, and I led the league in scoring four times. So you see I had nothing to prove, except to me.

I was not pleased with the way my career had ended. My last few years in the NFL had been uneventful, and except for almost helping the Cleveland Browns to the Super Bowl the game had lost its zing for me. When Jamie called me to come help him coach this young bunch, the first thing I thought was that this was way beneath me. My ego said, "Why would I want to help out a little town football team?" Well, I accepted, and after the first practice I knew why I was doing this. These young men were from every walk of life, and none were driven by anything more than their LOVE of the game. They only needed motivation and assurance that winning could be achieved.

# A Game Ball for Frank

At that time, my personal life was in shambles. I was going through a divorce but had just met my new love of my life, who is still the love of my life today after 23 years. We have nine wonderful children and 13 incredible grandchildren, all of whom love their Papa. To coach and play for the Generals became the greatest pleasure of my life. They loved football and absorbed everything I said to them. It became obvious early on that we didn't have a kicker, so Jamie asked me to consider it. I was 47 and hadn't kicked regularly in a few years, but it was like riding a bike: you never forget how, but I found out quickly that after a while you just can't do it as well as you once could. However, these young men didn't care. It was the fact that I was willing to try again, swallow my ego, and become one of them.

I came to practice and fed them all the knowledge that I had gained from years of experience. I became their leader! I was old enough to be their father. They looked up to everything I did on the field and off, from making tackles on kickoffs to kicking field goals. I had played with some of the most gifted athletes in the world, guys who had tremendous speed, size, and athleticism. These guys were not at that level, but none of my former NFL teammates played with the "heart" that these men did, for the sheer love of the game. They simply wouldn't quit.

Little did I know that that heart would lead us all the way to a National Championship. I'm sure that Jamie has mentioned about all of the personalities and all of the hardships (like riding buses everywhere instead of private charters that I was used to). The personal tragedies along the way. All the emotions and fears of the journey. There was so much. It was a great time. I began to see myself clearly again. I was in love again, really in love. The game became fun again. And we WON.

# A Journey of Respect, Gratitude and Redemption

*"Whatever the mind of man can conceive and believe, it can achieve."*
—*Napoleon Hill*

Many people have asked me what it took to put together a championship team. Certainly, it takes skilled talent, solid coaching, and a strong competitive spirit. The drive to be the best requires that you clearly understand what you want, why you want it, and the ability to share that with others in a way that draws them to you and makes them want to walk with you on that journey. Great things, in my experience, require a team of people to go on the journey together, respect and gratitude must be part of the equation.

Respect for everything and everyone was a key value for the Generals. We had a culture where everyone was respected because everyone mattered. Any organization, whether a business or a sports team, cannot be successful in the long run unless respect is given to everyone without exception. I was proud to lead a group of men who treated everyone with appreciation and respect for their contribution—whether it was the great waitresses who served our pregame meals, our bus drivers who delivered us safely to our games, to the police officers providing security for our fans at games, or people like Mr. Horner who made sure our home field was always in top shape.

# A Game Ball for Frank

You have to have gratitude for everything big and small. Growing up without anything always made me appreciate the little things. Anyone that has achieved any level of success has been assisted by others in ways big and small along the way. You don't win a National Championship without a great team of people – outstanding support staff, coaches, players, fans. You are grateful for every aspect because without any of one them doing what they do you cannot do your part, and things falter. When a group is committed to excellence that group becomes an unstoppable – and in our case unbeatable – team. The players thanked us for being a part of this incredible team and they were always grateful to be together and to be part of a once in a lifetime team.

Of course, many people are also looking for redemption, finding a way to heal a devastating wound or prove something to themselves or to others that has been left hanging, unresolved. I'm no different; redemption was vital for me. I had to build a National Championship team and nothing else would have been sufficient. Because of my background, and the abuse I took, I didn't want to be "good" or "fair" at what I did – if you want to be fair, go grab some popcorn and cotton candy at the "fair"-grounds and go sit in the stands and watch those who want to put it on the line. The pressure was immense, but much of it I put on myself to never ever hear I couldn't close the deal. I never wanted to hear, "You did fair, but fair is the best you will ever be." I wanted to leave no doubt, and in the final analysis I did just that. There were so many players like David Hughes, Eric Bates, Levi Frye, even Mark Moseley, just to name a few, who for their own reasons had to win, had in some cases never been in position to win it all. For some this was the final sports chapter and for some it was a cap to an unfilled career.

A great friend of mine, Tom Dozier, said, "After reading your book something really jumped out at me."

"What was that?" I asked.

He said "everyone in your story is broken."

I agree. Putting the pieces together that became the 1996 Generals also began putting the pieces back together in the lives of these amazing men who needed each other and this team. Earning the National Championship brought a level of redemption to them that was both awe-inspiring and forever life-changing.

Through stories and profiles, this book chronicles the Fredericksburg Generals' journey to win the American Football Association National Championship. It took a team to get there, but the story is also my story. My journey to overcome my troubled childhood and find redemption and acceptance taught me to respect others and be grateful for the things I have had at every stage of that journey.

The first section of the book, "A Game Ball for Frank", is the story of how my stormy relationship with my stepfather, Frank King, shaped me and planted the seeds that would blossom into the 1996 National Championship. The things I learned and people I met helped prepare me to coach a real team of winners. The second section of the book honors the 1996 Generals and profiles the players that earned the title National Champions. The third section of the book offers additional stories of respect and gratitude, profiling some of the key people who helped me on the way to finding the Generals.

One of the reasons I am sharing this story is to raise awareness of abuse and bullying. At the end of the book, I have some resources to help you, whether you are a victim, observer, or fighting to not be an abuser.

Finally, I hope you take away that second chances are possible, redemption is possible. With an open heart and an open mind, people can come together for a singular goal—and nothing can stop them when they are moving forward unified. Hate is a powerful thing but it pales in comparison to love.

Now, enjoy the story of a boy who overcame abuse and partnered with an NFL Legend to fulfill a once in a lifetime dream—winning a National Championship.

# A Game Ball for Frank

# Part 1:    A Game Ball for Frank

*The best revenge is massive success.*
        *-Frank Sinatra*

# A Game Ball for Frank

# 1    Where Do I Stand in This Family?

*Courage is being scared to death but saddling up anyway.*
    *-John Wayne*

Recently, I returned to where it all happened. A homecoming of sorts. As I sat in the concrete bleachers overlooking the field of battle on which I led my football team to a National Championship back in 1996, a broad smile came to my face. The smile was as much about where I had come from as what I had achieved. My Fredericksburg Generals were a Minor League football team, but there was nothing semi or minor about this group of amazing men. I was the head coach of a team that would capture the heart of the city we played in and garner national attention, both for who we were and for what we ultimately accomplished.

A few years ago, I was told that my great-great grandfather, Brigadier General William H. French, led a division in the Battle of Fredericksburg. He and his troops fought on the same streets and in the exact same area as Maury Stadium, where the Generals played. My thoughts turned to him as I imagined him and his men fighting for their lives on their battleground, aware that so many years later my troops would fight a different battle on the gridiron. I looked up to the heavens and smiled, thankful that his sacrifices allowed me to enjoy my successes today. I know he would be proud of me, because as odd as it may sound, I always felt a positive presence at Maury Stadium, and I could never quite explain it until I made the connection with my ancestor. Before I ever even stepped foot in that stadium, though, I had to fight some pretty intense battles of my own.

For as long as I can remember, I always believed in myself and my ability to do something great in my life. My mom always told me that I could do anything, and I internalized that into meaning the world was my oyster. I have always had a deep belief that I could accomplish things that would impact the world, or at the very least the lives of others. My hope is that by telling my story I can help others, and if I can then my hardships and all that I fought to overcome will have been worthwhile. Through my darkest periods, the thoughts of someday accomplishing great things kept me going. Faced with an onslaught of personal verbal and physical attacks, I discovered a gift called intestinal fortitude, and it drove my stepfather Frank, my childhood nemesis, crazy because he was hell bent on convincing me that I was a failure.

I have enjoyed a certain level of success, and I know for a fact that without God's divine intervention it would not have been possible. In my case it came down to a battle of wills, and I willed myself to not to allow Frank to win. I wanted to succeed, I wanted to persevere, but I had to find a way. Don't get me wrong, there were days when I felt broken and helpless. I dug in and continued on and made a vow to plod along.

I compare my situation to that of a football game with four quarters. If I could just hang on and keep it close, I would pull the victory out in the final seconds of the fourth quarter. "Hang in and hang on," I told myself, "and each day you will get closer to your goal." Could I be great? Would I be great? Would I ever achieve anything that would be considered a major success? As a young, beaten-down kid, I had nothing to hold onto but the personal hope and belief that I would prove Frank wrong and I would show him, someday. I would prove myself to him and I was going to get there. I just needed to go out and make it happen.

### The Story Begins

I was born Jamie Lee Richards on Nov. 9, 1964 in Bethesda, Maryland, to Robert Richards and his wife, June Donohoe. I was the fourth of four sons. When I was a baby my parents separated, and times were tough. My oldest brother Steve teases me to this day that my addition seriously drained the little money our family had. I know he can laugh about it now, but fortunately back then I was young enough to be shielded from the sting of his criticisms. My next oldest brother Brett was born with some form of brain damage, which caused him to suffer from epileptic seizures. My third oldest brother is Earl is not only intelligent but musically gifted as well and there is virtually nothing he can't do when he puts his mind to it.

The agreement between my parents when they divorced was that my mom would take Steve, Earl, and myself while my dad would care for Brett, who needed extra attention due to his medical needs. My dad ultimately moved to Florida with Brett while I was still a baby. My dad was gone, and little did I know he was never coming back. Before Mom and Dad reached some sort of child support agreement, my mom did her best to make ends meet working and raising four of us in a one-bedroom apartment. I didn't realize it at the time, but in retrospect I have no idea how any mother could handle four young boys in a one-bedroom apartment. It is beyond belief. I never remember hearing a single complaint from my mom; she just dug in and made it through that extremely hard time. That alone is one of many reasons that I hold my mom in the highest esteem. We were very poor, but at the same time we were too young to really know any different.

Mom eventually remarried a man named Frank King. Because Frank was an integral part of my life by the time I started school, I just started writing King. Nobody stopped me. Frank's entry into my life changed it forever – unfortunately, not for the better. Frank was a talented, hard-working custom cabinetmaker who worked long hours. There was nothing he couldn't construct with his hands. Ironically, the man who built things of wood all of his life was someone also adept at tearing things down. And it seemed to me that I was the one thing he seemed to enjoy tearing most. Frank's entrance in my life began a torturous journey.

### *Enter Frank*

Frank King came from a prosperous family that lost their wealth during the Great Depression. Frank had many disappointments in

11

his life. He was promised a pony at for his seventh birthday, but economic trouble meant the desperately desired gift never came. The loss of most of his family's fortune must have been a bitter pill to swallow and a major life-altering event. After the Depression, he joined the Army and fought in World War II.

Frank was a good athlete and a talented cabinetmaker, but his dream was to be a professional draftsman. He never wanted to make a living building custom cabinets for other people's homes. He beautified other people's homes and I'm sure watching his customers enjoy their big houses and their success was more than he could endure. Working with his hands was the absolute last thing that he wanted to do day in and day out, but putting food on the table and a roof over our heads had to be his top priority. Putting his career on hold for my mom and her children seemed to bring out the absolute worst in Frank.

He loved my mother, but he didn't love us. We were the wild card, the add-on, the proverbial flies in the ointment. I think he went into the relationship with my mom thinking, "I love this woman enough to take on these kids." Shortly thereafter, that thought became, "To hell with this. If I can drive these kids away, I'll have her all to myself." Frank argued and fought with each of my brothers on some level, but he singled me out to be the constant brunt of his abuse. Maybe it was my love of sports, rather than building things — the thing he valued most. He was my worst nightmare and the furthest thing from a true father figure.

Frank started his journey of physical and emotional torment with my oldest brother Steve, who ultimately packed up his belongings and moved in with my grandparents, who raised him from that point on. This arrangement helped Steve and took away some of the friction in the house, but it also raised some questions. I loved my grandmother and grandfather, but they took a special interest in Steve, and decided that they wanted to help guide him into becoming a successful young man. My brother Earl never said much about it, but you couldn't help but feel somewhat jealous of the fact that

# A Game Ball for Frank

Steve had the undivided attention of my grandparents and we were left feeling abandoned and very much as if we didn't matter a whole lot in the grand scale of things.

I also have vivid memories of Frank victimizing my brother Earl, who despite the abuse tried to appease Frank by helping him build cabinets or other things around the house. Earl could do it all, but that didn't stop Frank from starting confrontations with him. Earl was a self-taught musician, and Frank would talk about him behind his back, saying things like, "he's nothing but a long-haired hippy freak," and a vast array of other hateful things to hurt Earl whenever possible. Earl, by nature, doesn't show much emotion, and he never let Frank know he got to him. With his constant verbal barrage, Frank drove Earl away too; he went to live in Florida with our biological father during the last years of our father's life. That was something I wish I could have done too, but instead I stayed in my mom and Frank's home and prepared for the battle of a lifetime.

The lowest of the low was whenever he would talk and belittle my brother Brett, calling him a dummy, an idiot, or any number of other colorful monikers. I loved Brett, who had the hardest life in terms of his disabilities. He was born with a form of brain damage and suffered other obstacles such as frequent epileptic seizures, yet he still had to endure the cruelty of Frank's acid tongue. I would often sit and wonder who could be so cruel as to verbally assault a handicapped child – but Frank was an equal-opportunity abuser. He knew how much I hated him for getting on Brett, who could not help his actions, but he simply didn't care. I stood up for my brother and did my best to protect him as much as I possibly could. I could never forgive Frank for the verbal assaults on Brett, and for the life of me, I could never understand how he could go after someone who could never defend himself in any way.

From my earliest memory at age 4, I never felt anything like compassion or caring from Frank. My Mom and Frank eventually had a son together, my brother Kelly, and this caused an increase in Frank's abuse towards me. I willed myself not to ever give up or give in to the abuse. I was determined that Frank would not win. If I got beaten or threatened, I would live to fight another day. The verbal assaults were nothing I could ever describe. It infuriated Frank when I refused to give in to his abuse, and my determination to stand strong probably made it worse, but I had to hold onto some piece of control. To this day I will never understand how a man could hate with such conviction and go to such lengths to make a young child feel so unloved. It made me question my own self-worth throughout my childhood.

Where was my mom, while all this abuse was taking place? A lot of the worst treatment from Frank happened while my mom was at work. During those times Frank would taunt me with, "Mommy's not here to protect you now." He would follow those taunts with, "get out of my sight and don't make a sound," "you sicken me," "I can't stand the sight of you," and a host of other choice putdowns. I kept it hidden from my mother to keep peace in the house when she came home. She was my one and only protector and refuge. My mom was working very hard to help us survive, and unfortunately for me she wasn't around for the most damaging aspects of what I endured. Whenever she sensed friction between Frank and I, she stepped in and tried her best to stop the verbal attacks from escalating. Because of all the times my mom tried to intervene on my behalf and replace what I was missing, I was always so close to her, and she will always have my respect, love, and admiration.

One of my biggest regrets concerning my own father was the fact that I never had the opportunity to ask him, "Why?" Why did he leave me? Why were we not part of each other's lives? Did he love me?

I was angry, very angry, that he remarried. Angry that he had a new wife and two new kids – that he moved on and that my brothers and I seemed to mean nothing at all to him. I felt the pain of being unwanted, the emptiness in my heart, in every inch of my body. It was indescribable.

# A Game Ball for Frank

When I see parents hug their kids and see the pride in their eyes as they accompany them, whether to a movie, a park, a sporting event, an awards program, or any other activity, I find myself reflecting once again on how different my life was growing up. It makes a huge difference in a child's life. Even through the pain, it makes me smile when I see those parents with their children, knowing that the memories being made for that child will be good ones. I wanted my dad's love as any child would, but I also wanted his protection. I wanted my dad to say, "I'm here now. It's going to be all right and no one will ever put their hands on you again." I wanted my father's unconditional love, support, and affirmation with just a pat on the head or a hug. Most of all, I just wanted to know that I mattered to him. I wanted to belong and matter to the one person, other than my mom, to whom I should have mattered the most. I wanted to matter to my dad, but it never happened.

This has always been extremely devastating for me to accept. Dealing with the rejection and the pain of an absentee father was difficult for me to understand as a child, and even as an adult. And making my life even worse was the trip through hell with Frank as my tour guide. I was continually bombarded with Frank's unique brand of condemnation. I was told daily that I wasn't any good, that I was a "no-good, ball-bouncing, good-for-nothing nobody that was never ever going to amount to anything." Frank used every bad word and all sorts of colorful language to describe how he felt about me, and he went to great lengths to abuse me verbally just about every day.

Frank would drink at times, and his drinking made things at home go from bad to worse, creating a situation for me that was nearly unbearable. His specialties were screaming, yelling, name-calling and cussing, and he loved to do the threat-and- intimidation act with me as a way of keeping me down and showing me at all times who was running the show. He would often grab me and pin me against the wall by my throat and threaten me. He seemed to derive great joy from intimidating and threatening me, and his goal seemed to be making me to be as miserable as humanly possible.

# A Game Ball for Frank

I'll never forget how Frank's drinking led to bumping and banging at all hours of the day and night. It was like walking on eggshells 24 hours a day, seven days a week. The unwritten script in our home was, "Whatever you do, don't let Frank hear you." He would yell, cuss, break dishes, slam doors, and do everything in his power to intimidate us. I remember crying myself to sleep many nights, just hoping that when I woke up he would be gone. Unfortunately, that never happened. I cringed and flinched with every banging noise like I was a soldier on a battlefield.

My mom, of course, was a victim too. "Pssst, don't make any noise; he's not in a good mood," she would say repeatedly. I would think to myself, "When is he ever in a good mood?" She also told us regularly to stay in our room and avoid going near Frank. My mom would often cry at night, and hearing her cry would tear me up even more because I wanted to ease her pain.

I remember lying in bed at night being paralyzed with unrelenting fear. At any moment, I knew that Frank could start banging walls and smashing plates and turn to abusing me. He constantly made all of us feel like prisoners in our own home, and he was the warden. I thought to myself, "I won't always be small, and when the day comes when I am stronger than Frank you'd better believe I will push back." I hoped I survived to see that day.

## Coping as a Kid

In response to what was going on at home, I became a kid who was always on the run. I took every opportunity to be away from home. I stayed with friends who would invite me over to their house just to avoid going home. I would do anything to avoid being around him. I spent hours sitting out in fields or near a lake near my house, just crying, looking at the sky and talking with God and asking that unanswerable question: "Why me?" I wanted to be anywhere that Frank wasn't. I remember hiding in the woods and finding any place for an escape. Frequently, I searched for solitude just sitting by a pond or on a log or laying on my back in the middle of a field.

# A Game Ball for Frank

I just tried to find places that I could be alone with my thoughts of something cheerful, which kept me going. Imagination is a wonderful thing, and I used it to go places or imagine things being the way I thought they should be. The world I created in my mind got me through a lot of spots I never thought I could survive, and I am thankful that through the hardships I still thought that anything in this world is possible if you truly believe in yourself.

I also found a best friend who had many of the same challenges I had. Steve Carey lived just down the street from me. Neither of us had a dad around in our lives. Steve's sister Theresa – whom we called "Peanut" – had a brain injury like Brett. It was great to have someone to confide in who understood where I was coming from. We didn't have money, but we had a lot of fun together trying to do things that didn't cost money – going to a ball game or hanging out or taking a walk, watching shows together, doing a lot of the things friends do. We were able to confide a lot of things getting through the tough times. I leaned on him an awful lot for a long time, and he was always there for me, and I've always been there for him.

I have always loved sports, and when I was a kid all I wanted to do was play. I used to dream about being able to throw and catch a ball with my dad and him telling me he was proud of me. I knew deep down in my heart that it was nothing more than a dream and was never going to happen, but I so desperately needed to have something to hold onto in my mind. Frank always told me that all of the ballplayers that I loved to watch would never do anything for me, and that I needed to stop watching and dreaming. He said over and over that playing sports was nothing more than a dead end in every way possible and there were no exceptions.

I was an average student, at best. When I had the occasional teacher who took a genuine interest in me, I could perform well. One such teacher was Mrs. Betty Reid, my 4th grade teacher. She took an active interest in all of her students, and made me feel like I mattered. She made me feel that, even though she had other children to teach, that she was going to do whatever she could to give me a safe haven for a few hours a day, no matter the damage that Frank was doing.

However, I was always joking around in other teachers' classes, wanting to be liked at school to make up for what I was missing at home. I got in trouble often, since I was acting out as much as I was acting up, cutting up, and doing anything to make others laugh. I did this in hopes of being liked, but the result of my discipline problems was placement in a class of kids with behavioral and learning problems. I didn't belong in any of those classes, but it was only years later – when I was diagnosed with Attention Deficit Hyperactivity Disorder (ADHD) – that I learned the primary source of my school struggles.

When I was growing up, if you weren't getting good grades and you were having behavior problems in school you were placed in a class with kids that were, in many cases, struggling with far more serious issues than you were. Back then was there was no ADHD diagnosis, and if you were deemed a bad kid, the policy was to pull you out of the regular classroom. Between Frank's abuse at home and the bad influences at school, I felt like I was getting it on both ends, and I was growing increasingly frustrated.

To make matters worse, my older brothers were excellent students, and the school environment was easier for them to handle. This gave Frank even more ammunition, which he used every chance he could. I was his whipping boy in every sense of the word. I was getting paddled at school and beaten at home. There was nowhere for me to turn, so I did what I knew best. I just ran. Frank seemed to derive great pleasure in upsetting me; he actually seemed to enjoy my reactions to his mistreatment. I never felt like I could do anything right, and there was nothing I could ever do to make him happy. This caused me great pain, because as a child you want nothing more than to please your parents, and pleasing Frank was impossible. He made me feel unwanted 24 hours a day. I wanted to be loved and cared for, and I needed a father figure in the worst way, but it became clear that was never going to happen.

# A Game Ball for Frank

## *Sports Dreams*

All children have dreams of what they want to become. Some kids want to be pirates, policemen, firemen, or maybe play center field for the New York Yankees. My dreams centered on a different sport – football. I wanted to be a quarterback on one of the traditional powerhouse teams of the day – somewhere like Alabama, USC, Michigan, Ohio State, or possibly the Maryland Terrapins in the state where I was born. As I dreamed my football career would include a few Heisman Trophies on the way to a career in the NFL. I was going to play for my childhood team, the Washington Redskins, so that I could play close to home.

Dreams are never to be discounted. They have tremendous power, and that power is amplified in the life of a child with circumstances like mine. As I cowered in my bedroom, terrified that Frank would start in on me, my dreams took me places in my mind that I couldn't go, or couldn't afford to go. In my dreams I could be anyone, go anywhere, and imagine accomplishing anything I set my mind to. There were no beatings in my dreams, no verbal or mental abuse. In my dreams anything was possible, and no one could take them away from me, as much as Frank seemed determined to take everything else. This was one thing I was determined to keep for myself.

I believe that a child without dreams is like a car without a motor. A young person needs to believe that there is great out there, or at the very least they have to believe in the possibility of a better day. In my dreams I was the leading man, the star of the team, and the person who came out on top. I could do anything in those dreams, and they were a precious escape for me that gave me time to reflect on life's possibilities, no matter how farfetched or distant they might have been. When I was a kid I wanted to be Broadway Joe Namath or Terry Bradshaw – both rifle-armed guys who won big and did so in impressive ways. I loved Joe Namath because he had everything I could have ever wanted. He was handsome, cool, and talented. Joe Willie was loved by the ladies and admired by the men. He did things his way, and he boldly predicted that his upstart Jets would beat the favored Colts in Super Bowl III, and against all odds they did just that. When the Jets won that Super Bowl, it cemented Joe Namath's legend forever.

My greatest strength was my right arm, I could throw very hard and very long, and I loved the deep ball. I'm not going to say I would have been an NFL player, but I think if I had been offered the support, guidance and coaching that I needed at the time, I could have been a contributor to a college program. I had some athletic ability, but I didn't have the educational foundation I needed to do well in school. Instead, I did just enough to get from grade to grade. My biggest disappointment is that my inability to perform to a higher standard in the classroom kept me from getting a college degree. I let my situation dictate my results, and I know now that I should have found a way to keep my academics as a priority.

I wish I could tell my younger self that education holds the key to great success in life, and I wish I had refused to allow Frank's destructive influence to help derail my education. I should have never let that happen. In my dreams we had lots of money, and our family was like the perfect television families on Happy Days and The Brady Bunch. The reality was, there was nothing that could be solved or fixed in my life in a thirty-minute family show, but it was nice to dream and think that there were fatherly types like Mike Brady or Howard Cunningham in the world. I am by no means Sigmund Freud, but I can tell you that children need dreams. It gives them a powerful and safe escape when the walls around them are crumbling down. Books also provided me with a refuge – with an escape route from the endless war at home with Frank.

But thank God for sports, because it helped me deal with that sense of loss and with the physical and emotional pain of life with Frank. Sports have always been my greatest escape, because sports never let me down. Don't get me wrong – the teams I rooted for lost plenty of times, and that is a part of the game. But I always had sports when there when nothing else. I could listen to Sonny, Sam, and Frank on a Sunday with the Redskins. I could listen to any sport, take myself to that field or arena, and think about something else besides my situation.

Sports are wholesome, unpredictable, and compelling. To Frank the athletes I enjoyed watching were just guys bouncing balls, but to me they were great players who could make the impossible routine. I loved rooting for my teams and hoping the players would play their best every day. It allowed me an outlet, a release into fantasy before fantasy sports were even on the scene. I would have been completely lost without sports, because every day the score was 0-0 again, and every Sunday my team could line up and possibly win. It was a great diversion from the reality of my situation, but it also gave me hope because sports is filled with endless possibilities.

I played football in middle school and high school. On my North Stafford High School team, I played behind one of the greatest quarterbacks in our area's history, Mark Ryhanych. I first met Mark when he moved to town, and our very first interaction was an all-out battle royale. We were waiting for rides home from school as we were standing on the front steps of Stafford Middle School and we had the following discussion:

"You're the new kid?" I asked

"Yes, I'm Mark."

"You play ball?"

"Yes. I'm playing football."

"What position?"

"I'm a quarterback."

"Oh really? Well that's too bad, because I'm a quarterback."

He replied that he was going to do this and that, and I answered with a little trash talk of my own. Nose to nose, we had words, and we weren't going to wait until practice; we were going to settle it right then and there. There were a lot of punches thrown; some hit their target and some missed. I threw him in the bushes, he threw me in the bushes. After about 30 minutes of stalemate we shook hands and have been great friends since that day.

He didn't back down and I didn't back down, and we earned each other's respect. I would have preferred a sit down discussion (it would have been a heck of a lot less painful), but we were two kids wanting one position, and we were prepared to battle for it. Mark had a very good high school career and an excellent college career at Concord College in Athens, West Virginia, where one year he led his team to the championship game. I didn't play a lot in high school, because Mark was the starter, but working with him made me a better player, because no one threw the ball with the velocity and accuracy that Mark had. He loved to practice throwing, and we did it hour after hour and it made us both better.

One of the most painful experiences of my life was looking into the stands and seeing no one there. To see other dads hugging their kids or offering encouragement was often devastating for me. I was happy for my teammates and friends whose dads were always there, but deep down it caused me a great deal of pain. If I threw a touchdown pass or got a big hit or had a nice run, I had to celebrate with my teammates, which helped, but it wasn't what I was hoping for most of all.

Frank could not have cared less about my games, and as I recall he only came to one event in all of my days of youth sports. I was in a wrestling match in middle school, where I just happened to be going up against one of the stronger kids in the entire area. I knew from the outset that this would be no walk in the park. I always had heart and I would battle, which is something that I adopted young, and it has served me to this day. I just figured the one time I had a shot to potentially make Frank proud and earn a momentary shred of respect. It was not meant to be.

I battled throughout the match, as I always did, but was unable to make much headway against my opponent. Frank looked very disappointed that he had wasted his time coming to support me, and the loss was compounded when I returned home and he mocked me for losing. He made it a point to let me know that it was a total waste of his time watching a loser lose, and he spared no comments about my efforts or the battle I waged. He knew how to belittle you, and it just cut to the core how he would go out of his way to make you feel even more miserable than you were already feeling. It was truly an art form.

Sports gave a lost kid something to cling to. It gave me faith that tomorrow would be a better day, and it got me through some of the worst times of my life. Sports never abandoned me, and sports always gave me a sense that anything was possible and that the underdog could prevail. I was the ultimate underdog, but I believed that one day, somehow, I was going to be a winner. It's that belief that carried me through the darkest days I experienced, and it was my love of sports that inspired me and led me to believe that anything was possible.

### I Grow, the Pain Grows

When children are exposed to harmful things, the effects can follow them for many years, and for me that harmful thing was fear. I don't mind saying that I was fearful, but I never knew what I had done to deserve the treatment I was receiving. I remember the feel of Frank's hand around my throat, of fearing the overwhelming strength of someone I was unable to fight back against. His chief objectives were always to intimidate me and make me feel unworthy. He knew exactly how far to go without going too far. Now as an adult, I have no understanding of someone who enjoys intimidating a child.

I hate bullies. I hate the fact that so many children needlessly go through a daily form of terrorism in their own schools or school buses or neighborhoods. The sad spread of bullying to online cyber bullying has caused so many beautiful young people to take their lives needlessly. How tragic that they don't see a better tomorrow or a future of any kind. It is a terrible feeling to believe that nobody will help or that nothing will ever change. This has to stop. We need more people to get involved. You *can* change a life by stepping in and asking questions or otherwise getting involved in suspicious situations. Your action could save a life, and there is no greater hero to me than someone stepping in and making a difference in the life of someone who desperately needs it.

As the years went by I got bigger, so the physicality of Frank's attacks become more and more extreme as he was determined to keep me down as long as humanly possible. As it escalated, he punched harder and often threw me to the ground. He had to show his superiority, and he had to show me that he was in charge. No matter what, he was not going to leave me alone. He wanted to be that disruptive force, that chief antagonist, determined to do anything he could do to mentally, verbally, and physically break my will. Since his life didn't go according to plan, he decided that he would take this child, who had dreams and goals of his own, and make his life a living hell. If all went as planned, he figured that child (me) would go off the deep end.

I always had this despairing feeling that if my future was ruined, if I turned to the bottle, if I did drugs or committed a crime, he would have been satisfied. It would have justified his abuse. In my mind, I could hear him say," I always told you he would never amount to anything." The fact that I knew that he wanted me to crumble like a detonated building and fall into a pile of rubble made my resolve even stronger. I was afraid for me; I didn't want to turn into a person of hate. What if I turned out like him or if his way infected me?

Frank's favorite messages were about how bad things were, how life sucked on every level, how a positive successful future was not possible. It was draining to listen to, and I would be lying if I said it was easy to maintain a steady-as-she-goes approach when things were falling all around me. My hopes were to make it out of elementary, middle, and high school. I would think to myself that life couldn't be devoid of hope or possibility. Those types of thoughts kept me going and sustained me through the darkest days.

# A Game Ball for Frank

A grown man is powerful against a skinny kid who presents no real threat to him, and Frank loved to display his physical strength for my benefit. He often pinned me against the wall and choked me to the point where I thought I would pass out from a lack of air. Those are the times that chill me to the bone.

What if he squeezes a little bit harder, will my windpipe crush?

How much force can a windpipe endure before it breaks or collapses?

These should not have been the thought processes of a child of any age, but this was my existence. I lived in constant fear while trying my best to be a normal child, so I tried to put on my best face and not tell anyone about the abuse for fear of reprisal. I lived in fear of pushing the wrong button and setting Frank off, because that would lead to an explosion, and I would be the main victim. Fear was my constant battle, and survival was my one and only daily goal.

Why didn't I report the abuse or reach out to the authorities? I was smart enough to know that if you did that, they would place you in the state's care. Looking back, that is something that I should have considered, but back then I didn't want to leave the one person that loved me, my mother. Mom was not around for the majority of the beatings. She saw some pushing and some whippings, but most of the bad stuff happened when she was at work. Frank had perfect timing. He knew when to drop the hammer and when to back off. I hid so much from my mom, because times were tough for her too, and I didn't want to ruin her life, even though I never felt he deserved her. I didn't want Mom, the people at my school, or especially social services to know how bad it really was because I feared they would take me away from Mom. I did what I could to prevent that from happening.

Don't get me wrong, I thought about, fantasized, and dreamt about reporting Frank's abuse so that he would finally get some punishment of his own. The thought dawned on me: What happens if I get taken out of this house and placed somewhere else and it's not at all like the Happy Days family, or the Waltons, or Andy Griffith? What if, God forbid, I walked into a worse situation? While the odds were long, those were odds I just wasn't prepared to chance.

I was going to find a way to endure the beatings because I kept in my mind I wasn't going to be small forever, and I was going to be the one that pushed back. I just had to endure years of beatings to become mentally strong enough to retaliate. It took a tremendous toll on me, but I made a vow to never let him win, to never let him destroy me as a person and that one day the sun would shine in my life. There would be better days ahead for me, if I just hung in there and battled. If I could do that, I knew deep down that I would prevail. I would ultimately win, if I could just persevere. For me, that was going to be much easier said than done.

### Places of Refuge

Before my freshman year in high school, my mom had finally seen enough of Frank's abuse and took extreme action. Things had come to a head and become so brutal that I was nearly broken as a person. I was at the end of my rope in terms of what I could personally deal with, and Mom resorted to drastic measures. One night she declared to Frank, "I am sick and tired of what you are doing to this boy every single day. He can't do anything right and enough is enough! I've had it and I am leaving until you learn how to treat my son like a human being." My stepfather didn't respond kindly. It was a long, expletive-laden fight that went from bad to worse. My mom immediately took several of our belongings and we left to find a new place to live. Later that day we moved into a basement apartment of a house about five miles from the house where we had lived with Frank.

My mom made the ultimate sacrifice for me and I have never forgotten the stand she took that day on my behalf. It was hard because I heard her crying in the other room at night, mostly because of the state of the family but also because of the financial hardship, not knowing how or if we were going to make it. She meant the world to me. When she cried, I would go into her room to hold her and tell her that I loved her, and that we would make it together. I remember about a week after we moved, and you-know-who came to the door hoping to get Mom to change her mind and come back home. I was only too ready to greet him, and I had been rehearsing for his arrival in the event he ever came by. Mom wasn't home and I couldn't wait to deliver my message.

"What do you want?" I asked through the locked inside door. "I want to come in to see your mother," he said. "She's not here and you aren't coming in. You own your house, and that's all well and good but this is MY HOUSE. Not only do I not want you to come in, I think it's best if you leave now!" You could have fried an egg on Frank's head by the end of my little speech; the red in his face was rising and fast. He cursed at me until he heard noise from the landlord up above and he turned away, telling me that it wasn't over and he would be back. It was an immense feeling of relief to see him walk back to his car.

For one, small brief single solitary moment, I was able to do something I had never been able to do before – to make him feel as he had made me feel. I may have only gained an ounce of revenge, but I have to admit it made me feel better even for just a moment. I went in and laid on my bed and cried, but happy tears. On this day, the guy with the white hat had won. Black Bart wasn't coming to my town, and this was a victory for the good guys. My mom and I lived in that basement apartment for a year together, and through that time we grew closer than ever. Frank would come around to call and take her to dinner, and he started to treat her better. That was all that mattered to me. At this point, my relationship with Frank was non-existent, and the hatred remained. In the year living alone with Mom, I saw the enormity of her heart and I saw and experienced the care and love that she had for me.

The year with my Mom was a turning point in every way imaginable, and it helped us become closer than ever before. That one year with Mom was unquestionably the best year of my life to that point.

# A Game Ball for Frank

There was no yelling, no fighting – just a mother and a son and peace and solitude. It was the kind of home life that most people took for granted, and normalcy was really all I ever wanted. It also helped me prepare, because in the next year I would be moving to West Virginia to live with my brother Steve and his wife Peggy. The move to Steve's provided me with a fresh start, and the very best part was that Frank and his verbal and physical attacks would be at least four hours away from me in another state. To me, that wasn't nearly far enough.

I stayed with Steve and Peggy for all of my sophomore year, even though it was a tricky adjustment at times. They didn't have children, so Steve and I had to figure out if he was acting as my big brother or my father. But it was safe there and they provided a loving environment.

I made a lifelong friend in West Virginia – Steve "Red" Tokarcik, who is considered by many to be one of the greatest high school basketball players in that state's high school basketball history. Even though we only lived near each other for one year, Red taught me a great deal about toughness in sports and loyalty in friendship. Red was one of the greatest competitors I have ever known. He demanded excellence and he demanded that you give 100%, 100% of the time. Nothing less was acceptable. He had a hand in my development and hatred of losing, and I am indebted to him for teaching me how to battle on the court, as well as in any sport I played or, ultimately, coached. He always drove the point home that if you don't always play or perform at the highest level, you let your teammates down. You owe it to your teammates, your family, the fans, and yourself to never stop fighting until the whistle blows or the time runs off the clock. You can never let up in terms of intensity and effort. This was not a sometimes thing, it was a full-time thing. He lived by it and he played by it whenever he competed.

At the beginning of my junior year, I returned to Virginia so that I could go back to North Stafford High School. Mom had moved back in with Frank when I moved away and technically I still lived with them, but I stayed at friends' houses and with my girlfriend's family as much as possible. Frank had not changed toward me and we still had run-ins, but I was larger and stronger and more adept at making myself scarce. When I graduated from high school, I attended Northern Virginia Community College for several semesters, but financial struggles prevented me from pursuing offers to attend other college opportunities such as West Virginia Tech or Concord College on grants-in-aid. Completing a four-year college degree is still an aspiration of mine.

# A Game Ball for Frank

## 2    The Many Facets of the Sports World

*Always make a total effort, even when the odds are against you.*
    *-Arnold Palmer*

Frank never understood me. He never took the time, nor did he ever care to know the essence of the person I truly was. Sports were my great escape, but just saying that somehow minimizes it. Sports were not only my great escape; they were my passion. I love sports for many reasons. When I played sports I felt hope: hope for a better day tomorrow. Hope to be faster, to jump farther, and to throw harder to be better. Sports offered competition, where you could go up against others and prove who the better athlete was. Sports were, in many ways, my salvation. I could lose myself in my team or a game, rooting for the heroes of my youth and the heroes of my generation.

I grew up in an amazing time. I saw the greatest racehorse that ever lived. They called him Big Red, but you may remember him as Secretariat. I saw the great fights between Ali and Frazier. In 1983, I saw my favorite baseball team, the Baltimore Orioles, win it all in 1983 led by my favorite players, Cal Ripken Jr. and Eddie Murray.

I saw the great Steelers – with Bradshaw, Swann, Stallworth and the Steel Curtain – and I saw my favorite team, the Washington Redskins, lose their first Super Bowl but go on to win three more. They won one with Joe Theismann and the Diesel, John Riggins, leading the way with a kicker by the name of Mark Moseley. They won another with Doug Williams, the first African-American quarterback to win a Super Bowl, and another with my great friend Mark Rypien, who was the first Canadian-born quarterback to win a Super Bowl.

These were more than just players and teams to me – they were a diversion from everything I was dealing with. It was fantasy in many ways, but it allowed me a welcome respite. We were poor and we had no personal contact with any athletes; we just saw them on TV. A family friend once brought me an autographed black and white picture of former Redskins linebacker Harold "Tank" McClinton. It wasn't a personalized autograph – it was just a name on a picture – but it was as close as I had ever come to meeting one of the Redskins, and I loved that picture. It wasn't until I got into broadcasting that I was able to cover the team and get to know the players.

### A Taste of Broadcasting

My career in broadcasting began when I was a senior in high school. I started doing daily reports from my high school through DECA (Distributive Education Clubs of America, Incorporated). My teacher, Ms. Lois Campbell (now Simms) was a wonderful teacher: smart, spunky and full of energy. She introduced me to broadcasting because she felt it may be a great fit for me, and in so doing she changed my life. Thanks to Ms. Campbell's caring and leadership, as a senior I was named high school broadcaster of the year for reporting the news at North Stafford High School.

Another key ally for me was Mike Neville, the DJ at WPWC, the radio station that I called into every day to deliver news reports from North Stafford. Mike was always going to bat for me with station management, because unlike the other kids who called the station, who read items like the weekly lunch menu, the upcoming exam schedule or a school dance update, I provided legitimate content. I did interviews with coaches and players and I had other exciting features. I did more with less than you can imagine.

Radio station WPWC was located in Dumfries, Va., and was owned by Country Music DJ Hall of Famer Raymond "Cousin Ray" Woolfenden. As a small market station it had its budget challenges, but it offered me a great opportunity to develop my skills. Every Saturday morning, I helped Mike Neville to do a show called the "Sports Scene." We loved doing it, and it was an amazing chance for a young man to grow while under the supervision of someone that I looked up to for his professionalism and his talent. Mike is universally revered, and he is an amazing talent. The high school kids in the area who Mike Neville covered never got shortchanged; even if they were just a small-town high school athlete, he gave all he had to covering their accomplishments. Mike was an excellent broadcasting role model for me. He took heat for allowing a young kid to grow in the business, and I will always be grateful to him for giving me the opportunity to find my way.

I remember getting paid $10 a game to cover football or basketball games, which to me was BIG money at the time, and I earned it doing something I loved. I would have gladly done it for free, because I wanted to get better. I was making money talking about sports! I thought to myself that if I didn't finally make it to the NFL, I could always work in radio. I was a solid athlete with a strong arm, and I could run very well. I was "country strong", but I only lifted weights when it was mandatory. Lifting wasn't something that could hold my interest for very long, but broadcasting was a much different story. I was eager to learn every aspect of the business and was willing to make an effort to get around people I could really learn from.

### Tackling Football and the Minor Leagues

I didn't go to college to play football, and since I didn't get a lot of repetitions waiting behind Mark, I decided to play Minor League football for the Virginia Storm, which was based out of Woodbridge, Va. Is minor league ball a route to the NFL? Certainly. Johnny Unitas of Baltimore Colts fame and Eric Swann of the Arizona Cardinals both played minor league ball before signing with the NFL. Many others have found minor league football as a route to the Canadian league or Arena Football. Is it something of a longshot? Maybe, but it gives players who are looking to see just what they are made of another chance to test themselves and their skills.

I was a quarterback for the 1983 through 1985 seasons. I had a lot of heart and I threw the ball well. I played a lot early on and I took my lumps, including cracked ribs, a busted nose and other aches and pains, but I kept playing. I wanted to prove my toughness to my teammates, and playing with pain was one way to do that. I threw for a lot of yards and did well in the games I played. I was, and still am, ultra-competitive, and I think my teammates admired my guts and toughness.

I had a lot of fun playing. Our games were at G. Richard Phitzner Stadium in Woodbridge, VA. It was torn down in the late 1990's and rebuilt for the Potomac Nationals minor league baseball team. It was great to have the fans come out on a Saturday night. Things got rowdy and they enjoyed it. I always felt the fans appreciated my efforts. While I wasn't the most talented player, I had a lot of heart and I would give it everything I had. I would dive for first downs. I would hang in and take big hits and throw the ball and do things. The crowd paid good money, they deserved to see the best we could give them. I always gave my all. We didn't always win, but when we left the stadium I felt that I played as hard as I could for them.

I never gave up on my teammates, and I expected the same in return. My favorite target was my best friend on the team, wide receiver Tim Paolangeli, who was diminutive at 5-feet-9½, but fast and ultra-quick as he just had a knack for making people miss. One year when I didn't play much, we often drove in together and always said that we would connect before the season was over. On the last game of the season, and on the game's final play, we were down 17 in a playoff game against the New Jersey Bears, and on the last play of the game the defensive end was offside, thus allowing one more untimed play with 0:00 on the clock. I dropped back and juked a defensive end out of his shoes and rolled right, very much like the famous Hail Mary play of Boston College with Doug Flutie and Gerard Phelan. I bought some extra time, and somehow against a five-deep coverage where they were all dropped back to the 10-yard line, I let it fly from our side of the 50, The ball went 65 yards in the air and my Gerard Phelan was Tim. He hauled it in for a touchdown, which was amazing. I ran the whole way down the field pumping my fist, wishing that the score would have been three or four points different and that touchdown would have been a game winner.

Football is a team game, and so many people impact your life in so many ways. Our coach was Bob Shaw, who wasn't the richest man in the world, but he did everything in his power to make his players feel like they were something special. I learned a lot from Coach Shaw, and little did I know I would use some of those lessons as the coach of my own team down the road. Bob had an assistant coach named Carl Preginzer, who was a very nice man, with a great sense of humor. He had a heart of gold and was a great football man.

Our defensive coordinator Thomas Tate was a major impact on me. A 6' 3", 285-pound African-American Prince William County police officer, Tom had a booming voice with a very commanding presence. He used to make us all laugh with a silly joke that I was usually in on. It wasn't the funniest joke in the world, but to him it was hilarious and he seemed to find it funnier every time he told it. It went something like this. He would look at me and give me the signal that he was going to get someone with the joke. He would say, "Hey Robert, what's red all over and goes ding dong?" When the person asked didn't know, he would bellow, "A red ding dong, dummy!" Then he would laugh until he almost passed out. I guess the fact that we all laughed and egged him on to do it just encouraged him into trying it out a lot on unsuspecting people.

Tom truly showed me to love and care for others – that it was not a matter of color but a matter of one's character. Tom had a saying: "It's Time." He said it before we left the locker room and on the sidelines if we needed a big play. He was never afraid to challenge us or to speak his mind. In the locker room at halftime he would say to me, "Hey, number 12, if you get the ball in the end zone on offense, we will win this game, because they are not scoring again." He brought out the best in others, and that is what leadership is all about: inspiring and challenging others to do great things.

# A Game Ball for Frank

I had a successful Minor League career, and once I finally realized that the NFL was not going to call on me as a player I decided that if I ever got the chance, I would go into coaching.

## *Growing as a Broadcaster*

My work at WPWC was probably heard by two goats and some chickens down the road, but it was an invaluable experience. It allowed me to learn the craft from the bottom and work my way up, and before long I was able to parlay my work in the area into some local television. I became the part-time sports director at RCC Television in Fredericksburg, Va. The station was owned and operated by Thomas Seay. Tom was a very nice guy who had built quite a following of viewers who loved to hear him pontificate on all of the happenings of our area. Tom allowed a young guy to come in to learn, make mistakes, and try to get better every day. I wanted to cover big teams like the Redskins, and Tom always encouraged me to go for it. It was a great time and a wonderful place to learn with incredible people. Tom marveled at how I was able to find a way into NFL or MLB stadiums even though I worked for a relatively small news outlet.

To me, broadcasting was the most amazing profession on earth. Who wouldn't love a job that allows you to talk to the players, go to the games, learn about the strategy and hear the details of the big plays? To top it off, the working press usually gets a free meal, which is a nice perk. Granted some arenas and stadiums offer better food choices than others, but it was free, and I was always grateful for that. When I first started in the business, I couldn't imagine anyone who wouldn't want to cover professional sports. Frank hated sports, he couldn't grasp the idea of earning a living in the sports world and he tried to dissuade me at every opportunity.

But I saw it very differently. Sports always gave me an outlet, an opportunity to see that there are winners and losers in life. Sports was a direct parallel for me as I saw the difference between teams that prepared and those that just showed up. I studied great players and great general managers and coaches to see what made them tick and what made them successful. I had no father figure, so I listened to the great coaches and tried to learn something from them about winning or teamwork. I listened to the great players to discover what they had done to get them to the level of success that they had earned.

I went on to host several sports shows in our area, including shows that featured the Washington Redskins, the Washington Bullets (now Wizards) and the Washington Capitals. I was living out my dream meeting some of the world's greatest athletes – big names like Bo Jackson, Michael Jordan, Wayne Gretzky, Cal Ripken Jr., and many others. I produced, I directed, I ran camera, and on occasion I even drove the limo to pick up the guests. Talk about wearing many hats! But anyone who has ever worked in the business knows that many hats are often just the norm in broadcasting. I simply did whatever it took to get the job done. I had the bug, and I was going to put together a good show come hell or high water.

### Major League Broadcasting

I was having the time of my life broadcasting, and I often wondered if all of the work I was doing would open more doors in the business. Then, in the summer before the 1990 NFL season, I got a call from an agent named Ken Staninger. Ken represented Washington Redskins quarterback Mark Rypien. He mentioned that Mark had seen me doing some television shows and he would be interested to work with me on his own weekly show, the *Mark Rypien Show*, which aired weekly on the Home Team Sports network (now Comcast SportsNet). I was stunned, because in Washington, DC, it seems like the two most important people in the area were the President of the United States of America and the quarterback for the Washington Redskins. Most years, depending on the political climate, the Redskins quarterback was more popular, especially if the Redskins were winning. It was a dream call, a dream job, and it was hard to believe that all of the work – the blood, sweat, and tears – had paid off. I couldn't say yes fast enough. I was going to have a coveted opportunity to do a show many top broadcasters wanted.

When I first met Mark he struck me as a smart guy who had a plan for his career, and he stuck to it. Washington can be one of the hardest places to play in the NFL, as the expectations are always high. If you are playing well you are universally loved. If you are not, you are universally loathed. During Mark's career he was loved. It wasn't all wine and roses, and he had to grow into the position, but I remember how hard he worked and how he was always prepared to lead. The 1991 season was the stuff that dreams were made of, as the kid from Garrisonville was interviewing the best quarterback in the NFL on the best team in the NFL, and I had a front row seat to football history.

How dominant were the Redskins? They went 14-2, winning 11 games in a row that season. Their losses were by two and three points respectively. I don't think that team has ever received the amount of credit it deserves, as those Redskins were so amazingly close to becoming the second undefeated team in NFL history. Mark had an outstanding year. His 8.5 yards per pass attempt was second in the league, and his 3,564 passing yards were best in the NFC and fourth in the league. Running back Earnest Byner's 1,048 rushing yards were fifth best in the NFL. The Redskins had two wide receivers that went over 1,000 yards that year: Gary Clark (1,340) and Art Monk (1,049). They were dominant on both sides of the ball, scoring a league-best 485 points for the year while surrendering the second-fewest points defensively, 224. To top it off, they had a dominating +18 turnover ratio.

To say that the Redskins, Mark, and I were having a great year on the show would be an understatement. We taped the show at a local restaurant in the Fredericksburg area. The show got so popular that we moved to the Colonial Theatre in downtown Fredericksburg. The theatre was standing-room-only every week and by the time Mark and the Redskins hit the playoffs things had grown to a fever pitch. We marveled, traveling downtown in the car on the way to the show, looking at the lines of people clad in burgundy and gold all the way down the street and around the block.

We had a great time, and I felt like a good luck charm. It was working for Mark, so I think he wanted to keep the routine going, because it was a successful show and it was a very successful season with the best yet to come. During the playoffs Mark was in rare form; he would tell jokes and sing to the crowd. One night before the show started taping, he took the microphone and whipped the crowd into a frenzy singing Billy Joel's "Piano Man," much to the delight of the packed theatre crowd, which gave him a standing ovation. It was great to see and he really enjoyed it.

As the regular season ended, the Redskins were in prime position to win a Super Bowl. One of the best moments of the regular season was against the Atlanta Falcons. I witnessed one of the greatest days a quarterback ever had. Mark was on fire all day, destroying the Falcons secondary time and time again. His six touchdown passes that day, tying the club record held by Slingin' Sammy Baugh (accomplished twice, in 1943 and 1947). His average gain of 27.63 yards per completion broke Baugh's NFL record of 18.58, set in 1948. Mark could have surpassed Baugh's club record of 446 yards (1948), but decided to leave the game after his sixth touchdown pass of the game. He said afterwards, "You don't just go back in to set records."

We faced those same Falcons in the first round of the playoffs, and Mark and the Skins were on top of their game with a 24-7 win in the NFC Divisional Playoff game. They went on to beat the Detroit Lions in blowout fashion 41-10, which set up a Super Bowl matchup against Jim Kelly and the high-powered Buffalo Bills. Mark was brilliant in that game, as he had been all year.

### Heading to Super Bowl XXVI

One of the proud sponsors of *The Mark Rypien Show* was Billy Hoovler, the President of Communications Specialists, Inc. Billy is a wonderful person, and one of the biggest sports fans that you will ever meet. He is a particularly huge Redskins fan. There is one aspect to Billy that everyone who knows him knows and that is if he is a friend of yours you are going to get the "needle". He loves to bust chops more than anyone on the planet and he is an equal opportunity chop-buster. He loves to have fun and he has a great sense of humor. Billy has always been a friend to me and he has always supported me and my broadcasting career. He is a loyal friend and a first class person, and it has been an honor to have him as a friend. I am very appreciative for all he has done for me.

Billy told me during the season that if the Redskins made it to the Super Bowl, I would be his guest there. Well, the Redskins made had it and I was going to be there, and he followed through on that promise! I had always wanted to go to a Super Bowl because the majority of them were in sunny destinations with tons of fun. They could have played the Super Bowl in Antarctica and I would have gone. Lucky for me, Super Bowl XXVI was not in Antarctica – but it wasn't far off. It was in Minnesota. In January. Who cares about the weather; this was a dream come true. My favorite team, led by the quarterback whose show I was hosting, was playing the Buffalo Bills. I had all of the access to report from the biggest game in the world. This was turning out better than I could have ever imagined.

When we got to Minnesota it was freezing! Before this trip, I had never seen the entire dashboard of a car frozen—from the inside. We went to some great events leading up to the big game. All week I saw people walking the walkways that connected buildings. To avoid the extreme cold, the locals wore masks, like surgical masks, that trapped air around their noses and mouths to warm it up before it was breathed. I saw people ice fishing, and it was a unique cultural experience. I learned one thing: I am a warm-weather guy. I have great admiration for the people who live in cold weather cities, and I guess it's all what you are used to, but this was a cold like I had never experienced before.

Our hotel was in a small town near Minneapolis called Fridley. Most NFL teams have a Super Bowl pre-game ritual to take their team to a small town the night before the game, and I remember thinking, "Man, it would be great if the Skins stayed here." In the morning, I woke up and was sitting up in bed as Billy went out to get some coffee. He opened the door and said, "Hey King, you're not going to believe it, but the Bills are here." I said "Stop lying, there's no way the Bills are here." I thought he was just messing with me.

He said, "Take a look for yourself." I jumped up from the bed, stuck my head out of the door and there were Bruce Smith, Darryl Talley, Jim Kelly and other Bills stars. It was amazing. That was my start to Super Bowl Sunday, and it was going to keep getting better when it was time for kickoff.

Mark continued his hot hand, and through his stretch of excellence that postseason he was in a zone that few athletes experience. He couldn't be stopped, and the Redskins couldn't be stopped, and they beat the Bills that day in Super Bowl XXVI, 37-24. I was hoping that Mark would be selected as the Super Bowl MVP, not just for what he did that day, but for his entire body of work through the season. I knew this would be his crowning moment. It happened – Mark Rypien was named Super Bowl XXVI MVP and the dream for Mark, the Redskins, and the fans of the burgundy and gold had been fulfilled in grand fashion.

Several weeks later on the way to a victory parade, we were in the back of a car and I told him, "Man, this was a dream come true. It was an amazing experience for a kid from Garrisonville, Virginia." Mark said, "You did a great job and earned the opportunity, and you should be proud of yourself." I replied, "Thank you for the opportunity to work with you in one of the greatest sports seasons any Redskins fan could have ever been a part of. To have had a front row seat to the 1991 season was one of the greatest most amazing experiences of my life." I will always be grateful to the underdog quarterback from Spokane, Washington who gave an underdog reporter a chance.

# A Game Ball for Frank

## 3   The Championship Plan

*Today I will do what others won't, so tomorrow I can accomplish what others can't.*

   -Jerry Rice

T he year is 1994 and I am still a part-time broadcaster looking to make my mark on life. Life is better: I have married my wonderful wife Denise and we are raising two great kids. I see my mom occasionally – and Frank. Of course, he is no longer physically abusive, but he is still a force to be reckoned with in my life. About the only time we socialize is when I get together with him and Earl to play golf, once in a blue moon. We barely talked, but I was still trying to win him over in some form or fashion. I would try to crush drives, but ending up in the woods with major over-swings. Since I did not practice much, this strategy didn't work, and it left me open to his criticism. Frank would tell me all the things I was doing wrong – in golf and in life. There was no pleasing him, and so I wondered why I was even trying. I will never fully understand searching for a level of acceptance and respect from someone who in retrospect shouldn't have mattered to me at all.

Wanting to give back, I had ran a youth football summer camp at the University of Mary Washington for a couple of years. Leveraging my Redskins contacts, I had some great players like Wilbur Marshall, Mark Rypien, Gary Clark, and Mark Schlereth spend time with the kids. But I was ready for a new challenge. I heard that a retired colonel and business owner, Hal James, was planning to form a Minor League football franchise in our area, and the team was advertising for a head coach. I set up a meeting with the general manager of the team, a young man named Matt Kern. He asked me to meet him at a local Hardee's restaurant, which I thought was different, but I figured he might like that particular brand of fast food.

# A Game Ball for Frank

It turns out Matt scheduled the meeting for when he would be getting off of his shift there.

Matt shook my hand and I could tell he was super excited about football. Matt had unbridled passion and a love for the game of football. We hit it off as he talked about the possibilities. I have to admit I was a little stunned and didn't know what I was getting myself into, but as I sat and talked with Matt about philosophy, coaching and players I started to get excited. Matt Kern was a very important part of our team. Sometimes he took flak from some players who tried to test him because he was so young, but he knew the league intimately and was always there for any information I needed. Matt was truly like a Swiss army knife for our team, he could do it all. A diehard Minnesota Vikings fan, he is a sports junkie from the word go and he did everything for the team from painting helmets to keeping stats and everything in between. He would play a major part in our success.

After our interview, I dropped Matt off in one of the tougher areas of downtown, where he shared a townhouse with some relatives. I marveled at Matt and his ability to get along with all kinds of people. He considered himself to be just one of the guys and he was so enthusiastic. He wanted to win and he wanted to see the team do great things. He knew the area landscape and some of the great area players of the past and he was excited to get going. He wanted me to meet with team owner Hal James. Hal and his wife Raynor were a wonderful older couple who liked the idea of owning a team, but they also ran several businesses and thought a football team would be an opportunity to gain greater exposure.

Hal, Matt, and I talked. I shared my passion for the game. I told them that if I was going to lead the team, we were going to shoot for excellence – and that meant the National Championship. I discussed how I understood minor league football because I had played at that level. I shared with them how my sports broadcasting experience had exposed me to all of the great local sports talent and taught me how to see the heart, skill, and potential of players. And when the interview was over they officially offered me the position of head coach of the Fredericksburg Generals. Later, I was told that over thirty people had applied or showed interest for the job. Most of the interviewees talked about starting winning traditions and going .500 as a brand-new team or maybe making the playoffs. On the other hand, I talked up front in great detail about winning a national championship. They loved my enthusiasm and felt that I was the right man for the job.

As I drove home, I thought, "Well, you sold them on winning a national championship, so now all you have to do is go win one. With 350 teams in the American Football Association, that will be the challenge of a lifetime."

Before the first season, we had great turnouts for player tryouts, but in a lot of cases they were good players with heart but not "difference makers." Some of the players were great and some were not so great. And there were some, quite frankly, who couldn't play dead in a western. Our quarterback was B.J. Hawkins, a former quarterback at Potomac High School in Woodbridge, Virginia. He had all of the tools and was very solid player who played collegiately at Notre Dame, so we had a marquee name leading with whom the area fans were familiar.

In Year One, we played at St. Claire Brooks Park in Fredericksburg. Our field had a partially elevated end zone on one end. We had no locker rooms and no scoreboard, but other than that we were off to the races. I joked to the media that "we played before standing-room only crowds in that first season," which was true because there was nowhere to sit in that venue.

My mom was a great supporter of the Generals. She talked Frank into building a small wooden scoreboard for us. He came with her to a few games and they parked near the scoreboard. He even put some scores up on the board. It was the first time in my life he did anything resembling support of me. I wanted desperately to make them both proud, hoping all the while to earn his love and respect.

# A Game Ball for Frank

We went 7-6 in that first season, and I was proud to have a winning record for my first campaign as a coach.

## Hit the Road, Jamie!

As we began to think about Year Two, my wife Denise and I were talking about the challenge of building a winner. She stated the obvious when she said in order to be as great as you want to be you have to out recruit everyone else. I had already developed a recruiting plan, but hearing it from her meant that it was time to put the plan into action.

I knew in order to get to the pinnacle, I had to have the best players at every position with no weak links. If I could accomplish that, I knew that we could have a National Championship team. I needed to reach into that pool of talent I knew and *recruit* the talent, not relying on open tryouts as in Year 1. I grabbed Matt Kern and we went on the road like politicians running for office. I had to find the players and the player's girlfriend's houses – talk to the wives, talk to the parents – lay out the plan, and sell them on the Fredericksburg Generals. We hit the road so much and so often it would have made pro teams envious.

My first stop was at the home of one of the greatest running backs in the history of Virginia prep football. Eric Bates was simply electric; it was like you were watching a video game with the moves he had. It seemed he could go from zero to sixty, stop on a dime and give you change, and then continue on at the exact same rate of speed.

I needed Eric. I needed Eric badly, and something inside me said that in many ways Eric needed me as well. I went into my pitch on why he should become a Generals player. At the time, Eric had a child and another on the way, so he was hindered by the lack of health plans in the Minor Leagues; when players sustained injuries they were on their own to get treatment.

Right before me stood the key to my running game. He was the one guy that could carry the mail, as he had proven when he set many state rushing records. Eric was forthright and honest with me, explaining that had he not fathered a child in high school his life could have turned out very differently. He was heavily recruited by the top teams in the nation, and he could have played for any one of those programs. I looked at Eric and told him this was a chance to take part in something very special and that he would be vital to helping us win a national championship. He was eventually convinced and joined the team.

Our next acquisition had to be at quarterback. BJ decided to move on to other things, and I only had one guy in mind – my former high school teammate. Mark Ryhanych was, in the opinion of many the best quarterback to ever play in our area. Mark Ryhanych had the best arm I have ever seen to have not made it to the pro level, and I have been around a lot of NFL football. Mark was like me – ultra-competitive – which I loved, because he absolutely hated losing and he got fiery. If you recall from our first meeting in middle school, sometimes we clashed, since we were both bullheaded in some ways and we both wanted things done our way. This caused some friction early on, but we worked through it and he gave me the respect and opportunity to work together to create the most powerful offense ever seen at the Minor League level. Even when we butted heads, Mark and I would always end up talking through it and working together for the good of the team.

Mark was as natural as anyone you have ever seen throwing the ball, but he worked at it tirelessly and had a burning desire to be great. Mark's only drawback was that he was not a speed merchant, but he worked very hard to improve, running and working out as much as anyone. I will always maintain if he had been blessed with more foot speed he would have played on Sundays, and no one will ever convince me to the contrary. Mark was a competitor – one of the greatest I've ever been around. He could come out of the parking lot and throw for 300 yards, because he had the belief that no one could stop him, the attitude that all of the great ones have. He was everything that you would want in a quarterback: he owned the huddle, he was always prepared and he was a student of the game.

During the preseason, one of our philosophical disagreements led him to leave the team for a few days. But we made amends, he returned, and we worked through it. We never looked back. We both wanted the same thing—we both wanted to win. Those fiery 8th graders had leaned how to use that intense winning spirit to find common ground, and our mutual respect brought us back together. As a result, it was a ton of fun at timeouts to engage my high school teammate, the guy I backed up, and discuss strategy at crucial moments of games. It was exciting to strategize, and even more exciting to see it flawlessly executed. I knew if we could keep Mark healthy then we were in the driver's seat. One thing was certain – in order to win it all we had to keep Mark protected and upright, which was a major emphasis in filling the Generals' roster.

Of course, we also needed more skill positions to help Mark make fireworks on offense. During one of our player recruitment meetings, a young man came up to me and asked if I would be interested in a new receiver. He stood up and I realized that he was 6' 4" and had a very athletic build. His name was David Hughes. It turns out he was one of the best receivers I had ever seen. He played collegiately at Randolph-Macon College in Ashland, VA, and his addition was a major part of our success. We also added a speedster named Victor Horn. Victor was a speeding bullet at wide receiver, and when he had the ball he could go the distance at any time. With Vic on one side and David on the other, I knew I needed an offensive line that could protect and a tight end that could get open.

My tight end prayers were answered in the person of Tony Price, a military guy who was a natural wide out but played tight end for us due to our wide receiver depth. Tony was wiry and strong at the point of attack, and he could block. He did dirty work on the interior but his best work was as a pass catcher who was lethal in the open field. He was another guy who could make a house call at any place and time during the game. Tony was about 6' 2", and he had amazing hands and deceptive speed. He was much stronger than you could imagine. This gave Mark another key target that we always took advantage of due to the mismatches on the field.

Growing up a Redskins fan, I really wanted a tough inside runner in the model of John Riggins, and I got the closest thing I could find. His name was Levi Frye, he was 5' 10", 265 pounds, and he was built low to the ground. The beautiful part of Levi's game was that he was a battering ram who had amazingly quick feet and speed for his size. Levi ran hard and knocked many defenders out with his bruising runs. He told me the very first time that I met him, "Coach, one man can't bring me down." He wasn't joking; he was a powerhouse runner, and he knew he was a force to be reckoned with.

Next we went to work on the offensive line, and we built that unit into a powerhouse. My former Virginia Storm offensive coach, Carl Preginzer joined us and organized our offense. The offensive line was paramount to our overall success. The offensive line we had was comprised of very strong, very smart guys with a bit of a nasty streak. They hung out and ate together and they were very close. They were a unit that worked extremely hard. They opened holes for the running game and – most importantly – they kept Mark upright and clean and in so doing they allowed him to put up one of the greatest aerial shows week in and week out that Minor League Football fans had ever seen.

On the other side of the ball, I added a new defensive coordinator named Lonnie Messick, who had served as a Lieutenant Colonel in United States Marine Corps and who was the epitome of a "football man". He had coached at the Naval Academy and later went on to coach linebackers at Kent State. Lonnie was an excellent coach and a defensive mastermind who loved to expose weaknesses, and he loved to talk to me about how he was going to attack through a myriad of blitz packages. I wanted pressure, pressure, and more pressure and Lonnie wanted pressure as well, but he wanted to make sure it fit into his plan for that week's opponent. I loved coaching with him because he never got rattled, he never looked worried, and he was always prepared.

Lonnie was a coach that just didn't want to win – he wanted to dominate – and he did that every week. Because he had years of coaching experience, he helped me navigate some of the tough waters ahead. We recruited hard and he knew the type of players we needed on defense, so we went out and got them. Lonnie was tough in every sense of the word. He showed me how tough he was one time on the way back from a recruiting trip. We stopped at a seafood place and we ordered crabs, and while I was eating the small pieces of meat I looked up and he was eating the hard shell on the leg area. He was crunching the outer portion of a crab and swallowing it. I had never seen anyone do that before or since, and I left thinking this guy is as tough as nails, and he also must have a stomach made of metal to digest that.

Lonnie was a player's coach who would put his arm around a player, but he was tough, and he demanded toughness from that side of the ball. He was the perfect choice to lead the defense – he put a lot of time into game planning and he took great pride in making our defense the amazing machine it became.

Rounding things out, we formed our special teams squad. I recruited star University of Maryland punter Dan DeArmas. Our kicker was not only a friend of mine but a high school teammate. Ritchie Altstaetter was a both great receiver in high school, and an all-area record setting kicker, with a 53-yard field goal. Richie wanted to play as a receiver, and I asked him to kick for us as an extra duty.

On paper, I was slowly putting together what I deemed could be potentially become the greatest Minor League football team ever, and I couldn't wait to get going.

# A Game Ball for Frank

### *The Generals Express Begins to Roll*

When we finally took the field for our games, we enjoyed our new home on Maury Field. It was everything that St. Claire Brooks Park wasn't. As the home field for the local James Monroe High School Yellow Jackets, we had facilities and bleachers for our fans. Those fans packed our home stadium, Maury Field, every Saturday night to see an amazing aerial show with speed and power along with a defense that was dominant, hard-hitting, and relentless. Our defense reminded me of feeding time in a shark tank as they went to the ball carrier with all eleven men in pursuit, and it looked to me that they were upset if they weren't in on the play. It was a beautiful thing to watch.

My philosophy on offense, shared by my strong-armed quarterback, was run the ball and when you do that effectively, you set up the pass. Since we had the skilled people to do so, I preferred to dominate through the air, and we had the arsenal to do just that. I like speed runners and I like power runners and I knew whatever we called would work. We had an excellent offensive line that kept Mark clean, and they opened holes and gave plenty of pass protection. I knew our defense was in great hands, as Lonnie Messick was one of the most prepared people I had ever met. We shared the same philosophy of a tough-punishing defense that didn't know the meaning of the word retreat. We were a very tight unit on our first trip out, dominating the game and beating the Lynchburg Jaguars by a score of 18-7.

Game 2 was a thriller, coming down to the wire. Mark and I had a disagreement in the final moments of the game. I wanted to grind it out and run over the final few minutes while Mark preferred to keep the ball in the air. He passed the ball, it was tipped and it ended up in the wrong hands. We lost to the Richmond Ravens, 27-26. I'll never forget David Wafle, a former star at Duke University defensive player, who took me aside after that game and said, "We won't lose another game, I promise you that." We didn't know it then, but Dave's prophesy would come true.

# A Game Ball for Frank

That loss could have been a morale killer, but it actually ended up having the opposite effect. Mark and I were close enough to have a candid discussion. Mark has great instincts and nine times out of ten, when he saw something in the opposing defense, his decisions to stay the course or improvise was the right one. To his credit he is a gunslinger who believed he could make any throw at any time. You can't corral greatness – I knew he may have had a bad throw in this one instance but when you can do the things that he could with the ball in his hands you have to let great playmakers make plays and that's exactly what he did for his entire career as our quarterback. In this case, he needed to consider the big picture concern about time management – controlling the clock – and not giving the Ravens a chance to regain control. This strategic concern should have been more important than the opportunity he saw in the secondary. His call backfired on this one occasion. Our discussion strengthened our football relationship and after that game he was more protective of the ball and the clock. As a result, he never made another bad call.

## General Moseley to the Rescue

If we had one weak area in our program, it was our special teams. The field goal unit was not gelling as a squad. Probably the biggest reason was that Ritchie Altstaetter was very focused on being a great receiver, leaving little time for the field goal unit to practice during our precious practice sessions. It wasn't Richie's fault, as he had not kicked in many years, and it was a tough position to put him in, but the field goal unit as a whole just wasn't producing due to some timing issues. Ritchie was also a high school teammate of mine. He teamed up with Mark as one of the most potent high school Quarterback/Receiver tandems in area history. We all went to North Stafford High School together – Go Wolverines! However, special teams is a very vital part of the game of football, since so many games can come down to a last-kick situation. So, I reached into my contact list to and called the one man I thought who could analyze the situation, and perhaps advise me on how to coach the special teams. That man was Redskins legend and 1982 NFL MVP Kicker Mark Moseley.

Mark was a rare breed of kicker, as he was a straight-on kicker who was at his best when the game was on the line. He won a Super Bowl Championship in 1983 with the Redskins, and he broke records and did amazing things during his illustrious 16-year career. Mark had a famous single-bar facemask during his playing days, and he was always popular with the fans. I first met Mark during my broadcasting career, when he owned and operated his own travel agency in northern Virginia. I contacted Mark and asked him if he would come down in a coaching role to help us out in this area.

He agreed to help out, and he was on our sidelines during the first week of that season. One day after practice, standing by my truck, I asked him if he ever thought about kicking again, and he said he had. Seeing a golden opportunity, I said, "Why don't you kick with us?" He didn't say "no" right away, and I had already learned that he was a very giving person. I told him we would work within his schedule and if he could make it to practice, we would be beyond honored to have him. He was flattered and he asked if he could get back with me.

A couple days later he called and said, "I will give it a try." You can imagine how the sports fans of the area reacted. Through radio, TV, and newspapers the Fredericksburg Generals were suddenly on the map, because word leaked out that an NFL legend who had starred for the Washington Redskins was going to join the roster of a Minor League team.

Everyone met the announcement of Mark's addition to the team with a mix of excitement and anticipation. From his first practice with the team, Mark worked extremely hard with our special teams to make sure that we were in sync. When Moseley joined the Generals he was in great shape, and you could see by his tackling that he was someone who led by example, even if it was harder for him than for the guys who were half his age. He made the unit instantly better, essentially serving as a special teams coach and a kicker at the same time.

It was easy to see why he was such a legend – he displayed a strong work ethic and willingness for repetition, combined with his desire to be the best. During every game, fans would greet our team bus with Redskins shirts, hats, and buttons – all hoping for an autograph, picture, or handshake from the former NFL star. He gave back to the fans, our players, and to me in ways he may never know. His leadership, heart, and talent spoke volumes week in and week out. It was great to see a player who had achieved so much put his ego aside and help players see how a true professional conducted himself.

### The Generals Family

With the help of arguably the greatest collection of Minor League players, a dynamic defensive coordinator, and the rest of my first-class coaching staff, general manager, trainer, team chiropractor, support staff, stadium workers and the best fans in all of Minor League Football, we were on the quest to fulfill our National Championship mission. We were a family and we were extremely close, but because we had a veritable who's who of college and high school stars my greatest worry was that our players would struggle to check their football egos at the door. The key to our success was that everyone contributed and everyone enjoyed the success we earned. We were like a snowball going downhill; it turned into a weekly demolition and each week another victim got punished just for having the misfortune of having been placed on our schedule.

The best part for me is that these guys hung out together and did everything together. We were a family, which was of the utmost importance to me. We ate together at the Old Country Buffet as a team before every game. GM Brian Ellis and his amazing staff made sure the Generals were always well fed, and the service was incredible. Brian is a huge sports fan and he was a great friend to me and the Generals and he provided us with the fuel to go out and play our best. Brian made it a point to treat our players like they were in the NFL, and I could never thank him enough for those great pre-game meals and the encouragement he gave us. We also got strong support from Walter Dorsey and his crew at Checkers. A huge sports fan – the father of current Kansas City Chiefs General Manager John Dorsey – Mr. Dorsey donated funds for equipment, and provided meals for the players. The help provided by Walter Dorsey and the Checkers organization proved to be monumental in regards to us having the team that we ended up having.

### *A Year 2 Summary*

I had worked extremely hard to get the best positional players at every single position. We attacked both offensively and defensively from the opening whistle until the 0:00 appeared on the game clock. Domination was the name of the game: we were in the winning business, and business was very good. I remember going into every game thinking to myself that if our team was a card game, in year one I had a pair of jacks, but now I had a royal flush against everyone else's pair of sevens. Eric Bates did things athletically that other players could not. Every time he touched the ball something special could happen. You never knew whether he would leave would-be tacklers grabbing air, or break a tackle and go the distance. His dominance on the ground gave Mark Ryhanych options so that he could create a real threat with his incredible arm. Leading an offense with so many possibilities, Mark would light up the scoreboard. And the Lonnie Messick-directed defense kept opponents pushed back on their heels, wondering what hit them.

After games people would come up and say, "Man, your team is relentless. They attack people like piranhas at feeding time." It was like a Fourth of July fireworks show – an absolute joy to watch week in and week out. Our team was workmanlike in every way. Our players worked hard in practice, but everyone got along and chemistry was key to our success. We destroyed teams – rolling up over 30 points per game and giving up under 9. We had it all, and it wasn't a matter of whether we would win but rather by how much.

# A Game Ball for Frank

During our league championship game, a player broke out of the pack on a kick return and was gone down the sidelines with one man to beat. Mark Moseley dove and made a shoestring tackle, preventing a touchdown. The player was so upset with the tackle that he gave Mark a forearm shot in the back of head as Mark was getting up, breaking his fabled one-bar Redskins helmet. Our players, sensing that Mark was in peril, came to his aid much in the way a hockey team protects its goalie, and a near brawl ensued. As he walked off the field he joked, "I'm too old for this stuff." He was happy to do the kicking, but at the age of 47 the tackling demands were a different story.

The sellout crowd at Maury Stadium came to its feet and gave a standing ovation to a player that turned back the clock and gave the fans anther amazing career highlight to savor. "That saved a touchdown, Moseley said excitedly. "It busted my helmet, broke my face mask and I was almost 50 years old. I came to the sidelines to a rousing applause and admiration from my coaches and teammates and fans. It was something I will never forget."

We ended the year knowing we had everything in place to make a strong run at the one thing we collectively coveted more than anything, the opportunity to one day soon become Minor League National Champions.

## 4    Becoming a Champion – On and Off the Field

*Adversity causes some men to break; others to break records.*
*-William A. Ward*

From the very first moment I began coaching, I had one singular mission – to build a national champion. In three short years, with the help of arguably the greatest collection of Minor League players, a dynamic defensive coordinator and the rest of my first-class coaching staff, general manager, trainer, team chiropractor, team dentist, support staff, stadium workers and the best fans in all of Minor League Football, we fulfilled that mission.

We had no weakness, which is rare in football. We were intimidating on every level, and we had so many ways to beat you that I knew the only team capable of beating the Fredericksburg Generals was the Fredericksburg Generals themselves. It was my job to make sure that that didn't happen, and I am happy to report that it never did. I have a poster in my office that reads "Success doesn't come to you – You go to it." The Generals went to it and captured it every single week during the 1996 season, and it was very apparent to even the casual observer that this special group of men was not going to be denied in the quest for a perfect season and a national championship.

Naturally, Mark Moseley continued to be a fan favorite and a key part of our team. During our championship season, the one game that made our franchise was our 35-31 win over the

*Jamie and Mark Moseley*

# A Game Ball for Frank

Hampton Roads Sharks in Hampton, Va. The game was played in Hampton, Virginia in front of over 5,000 fans, of which more than half in attendance were wearing Redskins jerseys in honor of our General Moseley. Mark did wonderful things for our team. He mentioned us on Monday Night Football telecast while speaking with the great John Madden and the legendary play-by-play announcer Pat Summerall. He brought us national attention as we steamrolled to a perfect season and a national title. It was hard to believe that Mark, who I grew up cheering for and watching on TV as a kid, was now a star player on my team. I would look at him jogging off the field, high fiving me after another successful kick and think how surreal it seemed.

We had a tremendous fan following, and our games became the place to be on Saturday nights in Fredericksburg. Led by a 47-year-old former NFL legend Mark Moseley, it was not just a football game; it was a show. We had music and food and the fans really got into it, dancing in the stands and rocking to the music. Fans never left saying they didn't get their money's worth, as it was a happening event every week.

We scored so many points, on some nights, that I thought the light bulbs may blow out on the Maury Stadium scoreboard.

## A Frank Conclusion to a Championship Season

During the season my mom, accompanied surprisingly by Frank, would sit in her little red car on the far side of the field and watch. Frank was very ill with cancer, but even though he was too weak to sit in the bleachers they had a good vantage point of the game. Mom would always honk the horn and flash her lights every time the Generals scored or had a big play.

I was sensing that Frank was nearing the end. He had lost a lot of weight. He was gaunt and in constant pain. He coughed up blood on occasion and he could not get comfortable anywhere. I know he was there primarily for Mom, but I felt with the media attention we were getting that he was beginning to be proud of what I was doing,

though he never told me.

Each week they would sit and watch as he was deteriorating. I sensed the end was drawing near for him, and I found that I wanted to do something for him, to make peace with him. Despite the beatings and all of the abuse, I still respected him for putting a roof over my Mom's head and my brother's head. I had hated him with every fiber of my being for so many years, and I got to the point that in my late 20s that I decided I could either choose to live a life of hate, or forgive and be a bigger person. Please notice I said *forgive*, because there would be no *forgetting* what he had done.

We were preparing to play our final playoff game at home, looking to conclude our magical run at a perfect season to go (13-0). We were home against the Hampton Roads Sharks, which was considered one of the better teams in all of Minor League football. We knew we were the far superior team, but we had to execute and handle our business. We felt that we were ready to end the playoff by winning a championship in grand fashion.

I told the team and coaches that Frank was in poor health, and I asked for a game ball from our last playoff game as a gesture of thanks to him for coming out and supporting us. I asked Mark Moseley, who Frank respected as a player, to make the presentation.

Amid the sounds of the cheering crowd celebrating our victory over Hampton Roads, the team jogged over to my mom's car. Mark told Frank, "We would like to give you this game ball and thank you for supporting us through this season. We wish you the very best with your health in this battle you are facing." Mark then handed him the ball, which he reached out to receive, as he was barely strong enough to stand on his own. Then, the man that had been my nemesis, my tormentor, my abuser, and the one reason I didn't think I would survive my childhood began to speak.

Due to his medicine and the weight of the moment, his voice was very raspy when he grasped the game ball and said, "This is the nicest thing anyone has ever done for me." He went on to tell the team that he would never forget this very special moment. Then he turned to my mom, while the crowd stood silent, and said to her, "I want you to promise that when I go, this ball goes with me."

*The Generals Win it all.*

Turning back to the team, he said, "Thank you all for this," and he began to cry. Plenty of those watching the presentation were fighting back tears too, and many of the players became over-whelmed with emotion as they shook his hand. I had to step away, so intense was my emotion at that moment. Some people who saw me probably thought, "Man, he's taking this very badly," but it was actually the exact opposite,

I was overwhelmed with the emotion of the moment – the fact this one singular gesture had succeeded where a lifetime of trying never could. I cried because I was treating him with the love and compassion that I never received, but I knew that night that I needed to do this for me as much as for him.

The symbolism of him taking that ball meant that I was OK, that I for once in my life I had done good, and in this instance *I didn't need him to tell me.* I knew. It meant that for one special night the game of football, played by the team I had built from the ground up, had done something years of striving never could. For this night, that was good enough for me.

I knew when he took that ball that this was it, this would be my chance to let it go, knowing that I had finally earned what I had wanted my whole life – his acceptance and his acknowledgement that I was a good person. I walked off that field triumphantly towards my truck, quietly looking up to the heavens, knowing I just led my team to a playoff win that put us in position to win a National Championship, and in so doing I had just been able to put a much-needed end to all of the pain I had endured. With that night's accomplishments, I could finally begin to heal the wounds of a lifetime.

### *A Choice Between Love and Hate*

I knew Frank was getting worse by the day. He could not get comfortable. The pain of Frank's condition had made him even more irritable and I didn't want him taking it out on her. I went out and purchased a new recliner for him, but he only sat in it once, maybe twice. He was coughing up blood, which was blackish in color, and it was hard to watch on every level. Where I had hated this man so much, what I now felt was compassion. I wanted him to get better, to see the errors of his ways, and to somehow change. I knew one thing for certain – I was not going to let hate define me.

During the last week of his life, I stopped by thinking Mom would be there but she was at the store buying groceries. Frank was alone in the bedroom, and I realized this was maybe my last chance to get the answers I had always needed and to say what I had always wanted to say to him. I had rehearsed this so many times in my mind, what I would say and how I would say it. I wanted answers and I wanted to know why.

I had so many things to say, but when he looked up at me he was no longer the man who had battered me physically, verbally and emotionally. He was a shadow of himself, and on the spot I changed the way I was originally planning on addressing him.

He looked up and called me Jim, which was his way of being nice to me. I asked, "How are you feeling today?" knowing the answer but trying to keep his mind off of the pain as much as possible.

"Not too good. I'm doing the best I can," he said.

"Do you need anything?" I asked, and he shook his head.

I leaned against the dresser looking down at him, thinking of our role reversal and the power I had now. I was a strapping young man and he was in this fragile state. Despite the fact that the tables were turned physically, I still felt like he was somehow in control, and I needed to get to the bottom of some things.

"I have some things to say to you," I blurted out, and he cut me off right there.

"No Jim," he said, "That's OK. I know how you feel."

Incredulously I looked at him, and I said, "No, I have something to say and I have waited my whole life to say some things and I want you to know. WHY? Why did you hate me so much?"

There were tears running down my face. "Why did you do what you did to me? Why was I treated like that?" He started trying to say he was sorry for what he had done, that he knew it was wrong. I told him, "It never had to be that way I was never a bad person, but you treated me so badly you tried to ruin me as person. "

I felt bad about putting him on the spot, but I had waited my whole life to have this one talk, and it had to be done. He said, "You turned out to be a very good person who has accomplished some big things."

I said, "I want to know why...why did you do it? Why me?" I told him I would never understand why he did the things that he did. He had no real answers, other than to say he was sorry and he was wrong for doing it. I guess, in the end, that's about the best I could have hoped for, even though his answers left me feeling very hollow inside. It wasn't what I wanted to hear, not by a long shot. In truth it didn't scratch the surface of a lifetime of questions that I had. But it did give me a bit of the closure and respect that I had been searching for over an entire lifetime.

I told him, "I want to thank you for everything you did for me and my brothers. I know taking in four boys who weren't yours wasn't easy, and we always appreciated what you did for us. In terms of how we were raised, I'm afraid that's another story altogether. I can't say I'll ever forget what I endured and I hated you for so long, but I want you to know one thing…"

"I know," He interrupted, "You don't have to say it."

But I wanted to say it. "I love you, and thank you for what you did for me and my brothers."

I'm not sure where those words came from, but I knew that I didn't want to continue the cycle of hate that had driven him for so long. He never said he loved me, but that wasn't going to stop me from telling him. In this case, the person that was abused won. I stood bigger, I stood taller and I was proud that hate would not win.

With that, I took his hand and held it for a few minutes and then shook it. From down the hall, I heard my mom say, "Is someone here?"

"Yes, Mom, it's Jay, and I'm in here."

She came in and said hello. She could tell something profound had just occurred, but she didn't know what. I said that I need to be going and that I would see them both soon. I think I assuaged her fears as she realized that whatever had just happened needed to happen, but it was over. With watery red eyes, I kissed my Mom, gave her a hug and told her I loved her and walked out the screen porch and down the steps towards my car. I looked skyward with tears streaming down my face and I mouthed the words "Thank you."

# A Game Ball for Frank

I hoped God was listening, but somehow I knew in my heart that he had heard every word. It was apparent to me as I pulled out onto the main road that God had just played a major role in giving me the strength to face the one person who had caused me my greatest pain. Not only that, but to help me find the intestinal fortitude not to hate, but to have an inner peace and to find a measure of closure for the things that had caused me turmoil for all of my life.

### The End Game

Frank was laid to rest on November 6, 1996, three days before my birthday. Seven days earlier, the Fredericksburg Generals were named the 1996 AFA Minor League National Champions and I was named the 1996 Minor League National Coach of the Year. Many members of the Generals team, who had signed the game ball after that playoff game weeks earlier, attended Frank's funeral. That day Frank gave clear directions to my Mom that the ball was to go with him when he passed, and the game ball was indeed placed next to him in his casket.

As I looked down at Frank one last time everything flashed back, and I was overwhelmed with emotion as it finally dawned on me that all of what he did to me was over. He would never hurt me again, and with God's help I was able to come out the other side and accomplish something very special that even Frank was able to appreciate. On the ball, as I looked down I saw an inscription from star wide receiver David Hughes who had written, "See you in the end zone." When I walked away from the casket I felt ready to embrace my future, feeling that while I couldn't forget what had happened to me I could close this chapter forever. I afforded myself a measure of closure on things in my past that I once never thought possible.

There are scars that heal quickly, and there are some that last a lifetime. It was a journey that I wouldn't wish on anyone, and yet I found a way to survive, thrive, overcome, and persevere. I was a winner and a champion, and that was something that no one could ever take from me no matter how hard he had tried. Later that day, alone in my basement, I had time to reflect and I realized that all of this was over and that I had held true to the pledge I made to myself as a young child. He may have beaten me, but I would not let him beat me in terms of making me a person of hate like he had been. I fulfilled the promise I made to not let a person with hate take away my hope for the future.

Trust me, there were times when I thought I wouldn't make it, but I never gave in and I never gave up, and after all was said and done I displayed the heart of a champion, just like the heart that beat in the men who played for me. The Fredericksburg Generals were composed of a veritable who's who of great area high school and college players. The one common denominator that we all shared from me to Mark Moseley, and everyone in between, was that some of us were broken, some of us were in need of a second chance, and some of us only wanted one more chance to prove that we could be a champion. In the end, it was the unbreakable bond of brotherhood, a football family that met every challenge head on and walked away as champions, both in life and in football.

### General Accolades

The debate will go on, and some will differ with me, but I say without hesitation, top to bottom, there has never been a Minor League football team better than the Fredericksburg Generals of 1996. The Generals had won two consecutive divisional championships, and in only our third year of existence we won the most coveted prize of all – the Arkush Memorial Award, which went to the 1996 American Football Association National Champions. We were selected over 350 teams nationally to earn that award.

Shortly thereafter, I was named the 1996 Minor League National Coach of the Year, which was an amazing honor. I was recognized at a wonderful banquet in Canton, Ohio, right next to the Pro Football Hall of Fame. It would not have happened for me without a great coaching staff, the best players in the nation, great support staff and the fans that made it all possible. My wife, Denise, sacrificed her time running the stadium operations, making sure everything was taken care of, so I could go about the business of winning.

I know we were an absolute nightmare for opposing coaches, because how do you attack a team with no area of weakness? We were dominating on both offense and defense and Mark Moseley improved our special teams, as he teamed with former great Maryland punter Dan DeArmas to become the greatest special teams duo in Minor League history.

We had a mystique about us, a swagger that comes with being a great team. It wasn't cockiness; it was more of an assured state of confidence. We had great players that checked their egos at the door, and they pulled together every Saturday night for one singular goal to dominate and in so doing they became a team for the ages.

On the January 14, 1997, surrounded by my team and staff, I proudly shook Fredericksburg Mayor William Greenup's hand and then stood listening as he read the proclamation. My mind flashed back to the physical beatings, the verbal beatings and every time I got knocked down having to find a way back up. It was a tremendous honor and achievement that in so many ways was more than 30 years in the making. It was a long treacherous road, and I wondered if I would ever make it through it. I was proud as I stood there, proud of my tenacity and perseverance, which would not allow me to ever give up on myself. I saw a lot of me in my players – they never gave up and they never gave in. They met every challenge before them and won every battle in dominating fashion.

One final amazing thing happened with the Generals after the National Championship season. I received a call from Redskins Park, and they invited two of our players, wide receiver David Hughes and fullback Levi Frye, to come to Redskins Park for a tryout. We drove up there were greeted by head coach Norv Turner and his staff, who included Hughes and Frye in a workout. Neither was signed that day, but the invitation and interest alone further validated the talent level and the quality of players that wore the uniform of the Fredericksburg Generals.

The Fredericksburg Generals ceased operations after the 1996 season, which was fitting in a myriad of ways. I knew deep down that I would not be able to duplicate the talent pool and chemistry of these players, many of whom hung it up immediately after winning it all. The Fredericksburg Generals were a team of destiny, whose magical journey earned me a measure of respect that a lifetime of effort never could. This team was great on every level, and I feel strongly that the Fredericksburg Generals will be historically viewed as the greatest Minor League Football team to have ever played the game.

# A Game Ball for Frank

# Part 2    A Tribute to the Generals

*The only person you are destined to become is the person you decide to be.*
      *-Ralph Waldo Emerson*

# A Game Ball for Frank

# 5    The General Line-up

*I want Winners, I want people who want to win!*
*-Mike Singletary*

I t's almost impossible to believe that 2016 marks the 20th anniversary of the day I walked the sideline and celebrated winning a National Championship with the best players, coaches, support staff and sponsors. Most importantly, the best fans filled Maury Stadium to capacity, every Saturday night, to see the greatest offense, defense, and special teams ever to play competitively at the Minor League level. It was a group that was comprised of great players, but it was the players' collective efforts as a unified team that was second to none. I was proud that we had an offense filled with superstar players, but they all understood there was only one football, putting their egos aside and knowing that anyone could break one and go the distance or come up with a game-changing play at any moment.

Here is the complete roster of the 1996 Fredericksburg Generals:

| # / Pos. | Name | Comment |
|---|---|---|
| 1 / DB | Rodney Woodward | Great utility player. A super athlete a former top high school running back that we utilized as a punt returner, kick returner and on offense and defense alike very versatile. He was a real threat with the ball in his hands. |
| 2 / RB | Eric Bates | One of the greatest running backs in VA High School history. A human highlight film who could score from anywhere on the field. He could stop on a dime and give you change then proceed at the same rate of speed before the stop. Electrifying. |
| 3 / PK | Mark Moseley | Team Leader 1982 NFL MVP, Super Bowl Winner, Minor League National Champion, Minor League Hall of Famer. Inspirational in every way and the epitome of the word champion. The ONLY player to win a Super Bowl Championship and a Minor League National Championship, he retired having never lost a Minor League game |

# A Game Ball for Frank

| # / Pos. | Name | Comment |
|---|---|---|
| | | during his career with the Generals (22-0). Eventual inductee into the Mason-Dixon Minor League Football Hall of Fame. |
| 4 / CB | Joby Coakley | A lock down corner with attitude and swagger. He walked the walk and he talked the talk. He was a player who always made big plays in the biggest moments. He dominated the other team's best receiver every week. |
| 5 / P | Dan DeArmas | Former Maryland punter who teamed up with Mark Moseley to form the greatest special teams duo in Minor League history. He was athletic, and his punts and punt placements were a weapon that was lethal. He was a dominant punter who changed games with his ability to put the other team deep in their own end and he gave us short fields to work with. He was a game changer as a player. |
| 7 / WR | Bernard Ellis | He was a talented backup QB who could play a variety of positions and he contributed to our wins in many ways. He was a very fast, athletic player who could be counted on to produce big plays |
| 8 / WR | Chris Hicks | A hard worker who was a role receiver who always gave his best whenever his number was called and he pushed the other receivers to become better. He was a team first player who brought a winning attitude and work ethic to our team. |
| 12 / DE | Stephon Banks | One of the Virginia areas greatest high school players. He was a difference maker who played with a high motor and he had incredible instincts with big play ability. He was a game changer for us, and he always had to be accounted for by the opposition. |
| 13 / DB | Troy Spindle | A team player that always put the team ahead of himself. He worked hard in practice and he always contributed whenever his number was called. He exemplified the word teammate and he was respected by all of his teammates and coaches. |
| 14 / DB | Leon Gholsen | A kick returner who could score at any time with his breakaway speed and instincts. He could run and jump with the best of them. He was a rock solid defender who when he made an interception you could almost always count on a house |

# A Game Ball for Frank

| # / Pos. | Name | Comment |
|---|---|---|
| | | call that would follow. A true playmaker. |
| 15 / DB | Tony Talley | Tough, physical player who played with a nasty streak which he turned on whenever he played. He was a big hitter who would do anything asked of him on special teams or defense and he would come up with big hits and plays on a regular basis. |
| 16 / QB | Mark Ryhanych | He was simply the greatest Minor League Quarterback to ever play the game. He is one of the main reasons we had the major success we had. He was the one player we had to have and he delivered every week. The bigger the game the bigger the performance. He did things in the passing game that lit up the scoreboard on a weekly basis. A leader in every sense of the word and a Quarterback who was a winner who set the gold standard for the position. He ended his illustrious career as the Generals Quarterback with a 24-1 Record as a starter losing 1 game by 1 point in two years as the starter. |
| 18 / DB | Russel Williams | Russell retired more receivers than social security. He was a ferocious hitter who had amazing ball hawking skills. He had blazing speed and agility and he was a dominant safety who played the game with style. A playmaker always. |
| 20 / DB | Marcus Crawford | A solid player who was a sure tackler and who was tough nosed and was a contributor whenever his number was called. Very versatile athlete. |
| 21 / DB | Alvin Byrd | A solid contributor who always played hard and a player that worked as hard in practice as he did in games. As both special teams or DB he was always ready to contribute and he was a versatile athlete. |
| 22 / RB | Jeff Sawyer | A backup running back and a rock solid teammate who always worked hard and he ran with purpose whenever his number was called. He was strong at the point of attack and could run the sweeps effectively. He was respected by all for his team first mentality. |
| 25 / DB | Roger Bush | A very solid defender who was a great role player for the team. He excelled on special teams and as a defensive back whenever his number was called. He always supported his teammates and he always gave his best at all times. |

| # / Pos. | Name | Comment |
|---|---|---|
| 26 / LB | Carlton Raymond | Nicknamed the "Hammer" for his bruising hits, impeccable timing and the ability to produce game changing plays night in and night out. A linebacker who always played his best at a games biggest moments. A playmaker at all times. Eventual inductee into the Mason-Dixon Minor League Football Hall of Fame. |
| 30 / DL | Jermaine Green | Jermaine was a hard hitter with great instincts who always produced big plays. He excelled on special teams and on defense. He was a versatile player who always made big things happen. Super talented player. |
| 31 / FB | John Mixon | A tremendous point of attack blocker who could run inside and he would do anything we asked of him. He was a solid player on special teams and as a fullback. He always put the team first and was a key to our running games success. |
| 32 / RB | Morris Williams | A steady running back who had deceptive speed and who was strong at the point of attack. He was a key contributor who could run effectively both inside and out. |
| 34 / FB | Levi Frye | A bruising fullback who could get all of the tough inside yards and would provide bruising blocking for tailback Eric Bates. He cleared the way for Bates enabling him to tear off long runs and he always gained the tough short yardage needed for the Generals offense. He was one of two players asked to come to Redskins Park for a tryout after the Generals season concluded. He was a force to be reckoned with and it was an impossible task for him to be brought down by one defender. |
| 36 / DL | Trent Samuels | A solid defensive lineman who was strong and quick and he had a knack for finding the ball carriers and making plays behind the line of scrimmage. He was a key contributor to our defense and he could be depended on to give a top effort in every game he played. |
| 37 / DB | Jason Lee | A utility player who was a joy to have on the team. He was tough nosed and would play wherever he was asked to play. He was respected by coaches and players alike for his team first mentality. He hit hard and he loved to compete; you always knew he would give you all he had every time he stepped on the field. A true winner. |

# A Game Ball for Frank

| # / Pos. | Name | Comment |
|---|---|---|
| 38 / DE | Kenneth Mitchell | A dominant force from the Defensive End position. The former JMU standout made life miserable for opposing quarterbacks. He was a super smart very athletic player who had a high motor. You could always depend on him supplying pressure on the opposing quarterback through sacks or hurries and he had to be accounted for, often requiring double teams. A great defensive player for the Generals. |
| 40 / DB | Brian Cave | A special teams standout he was a player that maximized his potential and always played hard whenever his number was called. He was hard-nosed and determined, and he battled in practice and in games. He was a player that was determined each week to contribute in any way possible and he always gave maximum effort. |
| 42 / RB | Darme Marshall | A rock solid back up who contributed whenever his number was called. He was a hard worker and an excellent teammate who could block well and he also had deceptive speed. |
| 43 / RB | Willie Haskins | Another team guy who always worked hard in practice and a player who always supported his fellow running backs. He made the most of every opportunity and he was a player that could be counted on to contribute whenever needed. He had a great attitude and was a great teammate |
| 44 / RB | Mike Moore | A big bruising running back who was hard-nosed and who had great balance and who was very fast with excellent moves. He was someone who could make people miss, and he could also flash his power and run over people when he needed to. Tough inside runner. |
| 45 / TE | Dustin Buckley | A smaller Rob Gronkowski-type player; he didn't have Gronk's size, but he had his strength and playmaking ability. He could block, run like a deer, and in the open field if he had the ball in his hands it was all over as he was gone. He was a crushing blocker who ran great routes, and he made plays all over the field on special teams and offense. He was a true weapon for the Generals, with excellent size and speed, and a great competitor. |
| 49 / DB | Lee Yancy | A solid defender with very good instincts and tough defender. He was an excellent teammate who always worked hard in practice and he was a |

# A Game Ball for Frank

| # / Pos. | Name | Comment |
|---|---|---|
| | | player who was very capable of making things happen whenever his number was called. Versatile athlete. |
| 50 / DL | Chris Gant | A tough-nosed defender who was a solid tackler and a very hard hitter. He was quick of the ball and he was able to win his one on one battles consistently night in and night out. A real contributor on defense. |
| 54 / DL | Mike Scroggins | Hard hitter, quick feet, great instincts and for a big man he made plays all over the defensive line. He had a great attitude and he was a highly respected teammate who brought his A game every time he stepped on the field. He simply made plays all the time and he was a very smart player who knew how to beat his opponent. Eventual inductee into the Mason-Dixon Minor League Football Hall of Fame. |
| 55 / LB | Bruce Sumpter | A solid contributor who was ready every time his number was called. He worked hard in practice and was a rock solid teammate. He had great instincts and was a very steady defender. |
| 56 / LB | Michael Dickens | He called the signals on the defensive side of the ball. Smart, tough, hard-nosed, and a sure tackler. He was dependable and he was rarely out of position as he could read plays before they happened. He was a steady influence on the defense, and he gave everything he had every time he played. He was a big time player for us throughout his career as a General. |
| 62 / OL | Brian Hudgins | A solid offensive lineman who was very strong at the point of attack. He could pass block and run block effectively. He was a smart player who maximized his talents each night out, and he was hard-nosed as a player. |
| 67 / OL | Kevin Nelson | Excellent reserve lineman who was strong and solid in both pass blocking and run blocking. He worked hard in practice and was a respected teammate who always gave his best. |
| 70 / OL | Richard Mixon | Another solid reserve who had a great attitude and who worked hard in practice and who always gave his all. He was a tough competitor and he worked hard on his craft. |
| 71 / OL | Marquis Hamm | A tough guy who could block for the run and pass, and who maintained excellent footwork. He |

| # / Pos. | Name | Comment |
|---|---|---|
| | | was extremely quick and agile, and he was always steady and could always be counted on for big game performances. |
| 73 / DL | Robert Crawford | Robert was a tough defender, who made plays all over the field. He was a team leader and had the respect of his teammates. He was strong and always outworked the opposition. He was a difference-maker for the Generals. |
| 74 / OL | Lance Thompson | A strong blocker who was quick and crafty and who worked well with his fellow offensive lineman. He battled hard and would always give his best effort on game night. He could pass block and run block with equal success |
| 75 / OL | Dana Shields | A leader on the offensive line he excelled at the point of attack and he thrived in the game night battles. He was a strong pass blocker and he also opened huge holes in the running game. He could always be counted on to perform at a high level and he was respected by his teammates and his coaches for his consistent efforts. He led by example and he could always be depended on to play his best on game nights. |
| 76 / OL | Russ Helton | A fiery leader who would chant "toe tags and body bags" before every game getting himself into a trance like state. He was an emotional leader who loved getting his teammates ready for battle. His motor was always at full speed, and he gave everything he had at all times. He was all go all the time and he never let up until the final whistle. Inducted into the Mason-Dixon Minor League Football Hall of Fame. |
| 77 / OL | Tommy Fairfax | A workout Phenom he dominated every opponent he faced with his superior strength and upper body skills. He would lock in on a defender and they would be unable to do anything. He thrived on dominating the man in front of him and he created huge holes and was a huge success at tackle providing excellent pass protection for the Generals. Inducted into the Mason-Dixon Minor League Football Hall of Fame. |
| 78 / OL | Robert Pope | A solid reserve with an excellent attitude as he always put the team first. He would contribute in any way possible. He was extremely strong and agile and he made the starting unit better with his work in practice. Whenever he had his number |

| # / Pos. | Name | Comment |
|---|---|---|
| | | called he was ready and he always contributed. |
| 79 / DL | Tyrone Chatman | A tremendous defender who had speed and strength at the point of attack. He would make plays all over the field and many times in the opponent's backfield. He had tremendous instincts and timing and was a rock solid player for us on defense. |
| 80 / WR | David Hughes | A gifted wide receiver who had speed power and great jumping ability. He was unable to be covered in one-on-one match ups as he could catch the ball over the middle or he could go deep. He was a consistent playmaker that found the end zone with regularity, especially in the Red Zone. David was one of two players invited by the Washington Redskins at the end of the year to have a try out at Redskins Park. |
| 81 / WR | Kenny Nestor | A quality back up receiver who always was clutch when his number was called. He was a contributor on special teams as a holder as well. Deceptive speed and excellent hands; very dependable player. |
| 82 / WR | Victor Horne | Arguably the fastest player on the team. He stretched the field on a weekly basis and was a player that could hit the home run from anywhere on the field. He was a great receiver with excellent hands and he was nearly impossible to catch in the open field. On deep patterns when he got a step on the defender it was a touchdown for the Generals. He was a dynamic player who was a difference maker with the ball in his hands. |
| 86 / WR | George Jenkins | Hard-nosed player who practiced hard and was always ready to contribute. He was a solid player on special teams, was a solid tackler, and was also a very good receiver who had shifty moves and deceptive speed. |
| 87 / WR | Tony Price | A hybrid player who was wiry, crafty, fast, and super talented. He was used as a tight end but it was like having another wide receiver on the field. He could block as he was very strong, he broke tackles and he had home run speed. A hard worker in practice, he was one of the biggest home run threats on the Generals offense and he always made big plays. |
| 90 / DL | Terry Alazamora | A hard-nosed junkyard dog mentality. He never backed down from any challenge. He was strong, |

| # / Pos. | Name | Comment |
|---|---|---|
| | | and he was a sure tackler who was a consistent playmaker for the defense. He played hard and never took a play off. He gave his best game in and game out, and was a super consistent player who could always be depended on to come up with the big play. If you wanted a defensive lineman who would do battle and fight for you, Terry was your guy. He never let up, and he played with a high motor always. |
| 92 / DL | Steve Brooks | A steady, tough defender who worked hard in practice and was equally good at stopping the run and the pass. He was a player that was always ready to contribute whenever he was called upon. He was a very steady consistent player. |
| 97 / LB | Tim Torrey | One of the smartest players to ever play linebacker, he could diagnose most plays before they happened. He hit like a truck, and he had impeccable timing. He was as sure a tackler as there was and he was always in position. He could always be counted on to perform at a high level and he was a tremendously gifted player who got the most out of his abilities. |
| 99 / DL | David Wafle | The former Duke standout was a coach's dream. He could rush the passer with speed and athleticism he could stop the run at the point of attack and he was respected by all of the players and coaches for the consistent level of excellence in which he played game in and game out. One of the best I ever coached; he was a playmaker who could always be counted on to make big plays for the team. |

*The Generals Offensive Line*

*The Generals Tight Ends and Wide Receivers*

# A Game Ball for Frank

*The Generals Quarterbacks*

*The Generals Running Backs & Full Backs*

*The Generals Defensive Line*

*The Generals Linebackers*

*The Generals Defensive Backs and Safeties*

*The Generals Special Teams*

# A Game Ball for Frank

# 6  A Champion in Life: Mark Moseley

*It is not the size of a man but the size of his heart that matters.*
    Evander Holyfield

As a lifelong Washington Redskins fan growing up in the heart of Redskins territory, the name Mark Moseley was legendary in our area. Never in a million years did I ever think that I would one day meet him, let alone get the chance to coach him, but it turns out that is exactly what happened. Mark Moseley was arguably one of the greatest field goal kickers in NFL history. It is a mystery to me why he is not in the NFL Hall of Fame, since in 1982 he became the only kicker in NFL history to be named the league's Most Valuable Player.

I got to know Mark on a personal level, and he had a wonderful family. I am proud to call him a friend and it was an honor to have had the privilege to be his head coach and to watch him during our magical season. Mark Moseley wasn't under any big contract when he joined the Generals. He came down to help a team be successful, and his leadership permeated throughout our team.

Having been through painful moments throughout my life, I was saddened when Mark opened up and told me something very painful that had happened in his life. Pamela Moseley Carpenter, Mark's sister, was raped and murdered in 1979 in Livingston, Texas by Johnny Paul Penry, who was convicted and sentenced to death. I didn't know what to say when we talked about this, but I know his family was very close and they had endured an unthinkable tragedy. Things like that can often turn people very bitter on their outlook on life, but I didn't see that attitude in Mark.

At the time when Mark joined the Generals, he had endured his fair share of personal pain. He was in the midst of a divorce, and his once successful travel business was going through tough times because of major changes in the travel business. He ended up going out of business. Mark didn't know it at the time, but he needed this team more at that moment than at any other point in his life. It came along at the perfect time, and for a person who was going through one of the great storms of his life he came out of it to achieve his greatest personal and business success.

Mark would say in subsequent interviews that, "my winning of the (Minor League) National Championship meant more to me at that stage in my life than winning a Super Bowl Championship with the Redskins." Mark helped our team on and off the field, and he always told me that his favorite part of his time with the Generals was playing with a group guys who loved playing football. "They made football fun again," he said.

In fact, the Generals offered Moseley a second chance at life; much like the team did for all of our players. "I don't think my life changed, I think it just got more fun to enjoy it," Moseley explained. "Working with the team gave me new life that I had forgotten I had in me. My personal life was in a rut, and I needed to be reminded that I was still human, with the same feelings and emotions that everyone else had. I started living again. My wonderful wife of today, Sandy, came into my life about that time and I could see clearly again."

But it didn't come without challenges for the player that played for four NFL teams–Philadelphia, Houston, Washington and Cleveland. "Most of my challenges at 47 were physical," he said. "I just wasn't able to kick 50 or 60-yard field goals any more. I could still kick them straight though. It was making those bruising tackles on kickoffs that became a problem. Guys had trouble staying in their lanes on kickoff, and I couldn't be a coward and not fill the holes and make the tackle. But it was fun. The guys were great."

Moseley attempted to put in perspective his terrific run with the Generals in Fredericksburg.

# A Game Ball for Frank

"Having played football for most of my life, I loved the game," he said. "As a professional, the game had lost its excitement because there was always so much pressure to never miss, never lose. The fun had been taken away. I still loved playing but for a different reason – making the money. I had played with guys in the NFL who were some of the most talented and gifted athletes in the world, and they played hard every week but something was missing. These kids showed me what was missing: HEART."

Moseley said that feeling even carried over to sports' greatest stage, the Super Bowl. "With the Generals, I was starting a new chapter in my life," he said. "Life after football. I wasn't sure what that was going to be yet. I had tried several things, but nothing was really filling that hole, and playing helped me clear my head. Winning Super Bowls was great because of the enormity of the stage. It was huge, and the pomp and circumstance of the Super Bowl takes a lot out of the glamour of the actual game.

"The Generals' championship had all that, but in a smaller way, it had the real feel of what American football in my home town in Texas was like. I had done everything in the NFL that a kicker could do – won almost every award, every record. Played for a great team with great players, great coaches, but I still wasn't fulfilled with my results. The Generals' championship allowed me to finish at the top of the world. It helped me help these young men to reach something in their lives that they probably never could have by themselves by giving them the confidence to go out into the real world with determination, dedication to bettering themselves and their families."

Mark was an ambassador for Minor League football, and he and remains the only athlete in the history of major league sports to win a Major League MVP award and a Minor League National Championship.

How much did Mark mean to the Generals? There is no way I can adequately put into words what he meant to our success in ways both seen and unseen. I value his friendship tremendously. In the hearts and minds of our coaches, players, fans, and me, he is a Hall of Famer on every level, and that will never change.

What did Mark mean to us in regards to the leadership he provided for the Generals? We were a perfect 22-0 with Mark Moseley in the lineup – we never lost a game – and for me that says everything you need to know about one of the greatest kickers in NFL history. I would do anything for Mark, and it is my hope that he one day he will take his rightful place in Canton, Ohio – home of the NFL Hall of Fame.

In my opinion if anyone ever deserved to be inducted into the Pro Football Hall of Fame, not only for his contributions while playing in the NFL, but also for assisting future generations to know, love, and respect the game of football, Mark Moseley should be a member. No one has ever had the dual success that he had on two vastly different sports landscapes, and that is a testament to the man who set the standard and accomplished something never before achieved in the history of sports.

## 7  Childhood Friend, Competitor, and On-Field General: Mark Ryhanych

*If you aren't going all the way, why go at all?*
    -Joe Namath

My friendship with Mark Ryhanych got off to an unlikely start. Our first meeting in the eighth grade was a case of two alpha males not giving an inch to each other. He didn't back down and I didn't back down, and we earned each other's respect. Mark had a very good high school career and an excellent college career at Concord College in Athens, West Virginia, where one year he led his team to the championship game. While he led me on the field in high school, ironically I would coach him as he led the Fredericksburg Generals to the national championship. I got to share one of the greatest accomplishments of my life with one of my closest friends it was extremely special on so many levels.

Mark currently lives in Virginia Beach and he works for Huttig Building Products. Mark Ryhanych is widely considered the best Minor League QB to ever play the game. He was 24-1 as a starter in two years with the Generals, losing only one game by one point in two years. He finished the 1996 season with 3,097 yards passing and 39 touchdowns.

## 8   Defensive General: Lonnie Messick

*Failure Is Not An Option*
   *-Gene Kranz*

Defensively, Lonnie Messick was an amazing leader. He led a defense in his image – tough, hardnosed and disciplined. He didn't want to give up an inch of field position. He took a defense of talented individuals and turned it into a defense that had one mission and that was to seek, search, and destroy. He was essential to the success of the team, and he made it a point to dominate defensively on a weekly basis. In so doing, he helped bring a National Championship to the Generals and the City of Fredericksburg.

At times I would ask him for more pressure and he would invariably say, "I got you, coach," or, "Here it comes, coach." With his military background, he always had a plan and demanded that his players be physical at the point of attack, that they blitz when he sent them but that they always maintain position integrity so they wouldn't be caught out of position. He loved them when they played to his expectations, which was the majority of the time, but he would chew them out if they failed to play the way he thought they should. I loved the way he coached and he had a great influence on me.

I would go to his house, and he always had his clicker watching game film or he would draw up defenses and tell me what he was going to do. He had a look on his face when he had special blitz packages or certain scheme for that particular week. He had that Cheshire cat smile when he would tell me, "Coach, wait until they see what I'm going to send their way this week." As usual, he was right on the money, because he was so advanced in his thinking and preparation he had the answers to the test before the test was handed out.

We wouldn't have a National Championship without Lonnie Messick and I've told him that many times, but I'll do it again here: Thank you for leading the Generals defense to do things that no Minor League football team had ever done before. You were an amazing defensive coordinator, and it was an honor to coach with you.

He is still coaching football, at Rapid City Central High School in South Dakota as the defensive coordinator, and I'm sure tonight he's probably watching game film or thinking of ways to blitz or create havoc on an offense somewhere. He enjoys nothing more than dominating on defense – that is something I was witness to every time we took the field.

## 9  A General Review

*You were born to be a player, you were meant to be here, this moment is yours.*
*-Herb Brooks*

Here is an update on some of the other key figures who made Minor League history in 1996:

- **No. 2 Running Back Eric Bates:** One of the greatest running backs in high school football history, Bates was a human-highlight film any time he touched the ball. He made people miss with his electrifying cuts combined with his home run speed.

He was tough, durable and a game breaker who provided the offense with a potential to score from anywhere on the field due to his outstanding ability as a playmaker. Eric lives in Fredericksburg and is the father of five children – three daughters and two sons. Eric is a product handler for a food distribution company called Greencore.

- **No. 4 Defensive Back Joby Coakley:** Coakley was a shutdown corner who thrived on bump-and-run or man coverage. He was an in your face defender who had great speed and instincts. Joby was a very hard hitter who could effectively blitz, and he locked down the opposing feature receiver down week in and week out. When he picked off a pass his blazing speed kicked in and you could guarantee he was gone for six. If the opposition chose to talk they fell right into his hands, and it was over. Joby currently works for J. Barber Moving & Storage, in charge of quality control. He is still with his daughter's mom, Susan, and their daughter Keana, is 20 in her third year of college. He also referees at the Fredericksburg Fieldhouse.

- **No. 26 Linebacker Carlton Raymond:** As a linebacker, Raymond was a punishing tackler with a great sense of timing. He could read plays and he was always in position. He was a playmaker who always came up with a big sack, fumble recovery, or interception when it was needed most. He was nicknamed the "Hammer" because of the power of his hits. He could change a game at any point and was always a big play threat. He was inducted in the Mason Dixon Hall of Fame in 2009. He currently works at FedEx Ground in Chantilly, Va., and he has worked with Rappahannock Valley Football Officials since 2010.

- **No. 34 Fullback Levi Frye:** Former Washington Post sports writer Mike Wise said it best when he said that Frye, a 6-0, 265-pound battering ram fullback, ran like "a runaway beer truck with a broken brake." Frye was a bruising runner with great speed and balance who punished anyone in his way with his running style. Levi keeps busy raising his 13-year-old son; he resides in Woodbridge, Va. He is employed by Prince William County as an Intensive Pretrial Officer for High-Risk Youth. He was one of two Generals players invited to Redskins Park for a tryout with the team.

- **No. 37 Defensive Back Jason Lee:** Jason was a great utility player who excelled on special teams and also in any number of defensive back positions he was called upon to play. He was a smart, instinctual player who knew the defense and would do anything and everything to contribute every week. He was a joy to coach, as he had a hard-nosed style, but he was the consummate teammate. For a while he worked for the White House as a member of the United States Army, where he served as the Audio Visual Communications Specialist at the White House Communications Agency. He currently works for Strategic Alliances in the Greensboro/Winston-Salem area of North Carolina.

- **No. 76 Offensive Lineman Russ Helton:** Russ was a stalwart on the offensive line, and he was an emotional leader for the Generals. He was known to inspire teammates and fans alike with his chant of "Toe Tags and Body Bags" before, during, and after Generals games. One of the most intense players to ever wear a Generals uniform, Helton was a rock solid offensive lineman who dominated at the point of attack. He could pass block and run block with equal success. Russ is the current Director of Facilities and Maintenance for Manassas City Schools. He is married with two boys and a girl. He loved the unity and diversity of the Generals and the sense of family and togetherness that he shared with his teammates. "That was a special group of men that accomplished great things together, and those friendships and relationships that were developed will always mean the world to me," he said.

- **No. 80 Wide Receiver David Hughes:** David is a First Lieutenant in the United States Army Reserve with the 80th Training

Command. He has been deployed twice in support of Operation Enduring Freedom (Afghanistan & Kuwait). He currently lives in Spotsylvania, Va. with his wife Cynthia. They have two daughters. David Hughes was the other player invited by the Washington Redskins to try out at Redskins Park at the conclusion of the 1996 National Championship Season.

# A Game Ball for Frank

# Part 3 – Stories of Respect and Gratitude

*There are only two options regarding commitment. You're either IN or you are OUT. There is no such thing as life in between.*
    *-Pat Riley*

# A Game Ball for Frank

## 10    The Underdog Who Gave This Underdog a Chance: Mark Rypien

*The difference between a successful person and others is not a lack of strength, not a lack of knowledge, but rather a lack of will*
    *-Vince Lombardi*

I can't overstate the significance of one phone call on my life journey. Ken Staniner's call to invite me to join the *Mark Rypien Show* would give me a front row seat to sports history, watching my favorite team while becoming close friends with the quarterback who would lead us to a Super Bowl championship. I am forever grateful that Mark Rypien would give an unknown upstart broadcaster from Garrisonville, Va. the break of a lifetime. I have known Mark Rypien for 25 years, and you would be hard pressed to ever find a higher quality person. He has always been a man of the highest character and integrity. Mark and his brothers were great athletes, and there are great athletes throughout the Rypien family.

I've seen Mark on top of the world, and sadly at the bottom as well. I've seen him devastated by the loss of his son Andrew, who was only three years old, to complications from a brain tumor. No parent should have to experience something that devastating. When Andrew passed, Mark did something amazing; he started the Rypien Foundation to help all other children who are dealing with childhood cancer. Mark made it his mission

**Mark Rypien and Jamie, 1991**

to help others, and he and his foundation continue to do amazing work to this day. Mark is a true friend who cares for others; when my mother passed away in April 2014 he reached out to me with words of encouragement, and his kind words meant the world to me at the most difficult time of my life.

Mark and I remain friends to this day. In a world that often focuses on the bad that athletes do, Mark Rypien is a shining example of a person who has reached the mountaintop but has always remained true to his roots. He's a class act and a one-of-a-kind person who gave me a chance when I needed something good to take my mind of all of the bad in my past. Mark Rypien is a Super Bowl MVP, and I am proud of everything he has accomplished in the NFL and for his dedication in helping thousands more through his foundation. He was a great football player, but he is an even greater person, and I value his friendship and am thankful to him for the positive impact he has had on my life.

# 11   Teachers Make a Difference, Part 1: Betty Reid

*Winners Are Not Those Who Never Fail, But Those Who Never Quit*
  *-Edwin Louis Cole*

In elementary school I was an average student, not a great one, but I always seemed to do better in classes where I received some attention and some tender loving care. If a teacher was cold to me or was not a nurturing type of person, I would zone out, tune out, and withdraw. If I was in a class with someone who cared and treated me well, I would usually respond to them and perform well. One teacher stood out above all of the rest, helping to make my life bearable and giving me reason to believe that things would one day be OK for me. Mrs. Betty Reid, my fourth-grade teacher, was a guardian angel to me when I was a child, and she has remained a favorite of mine for more than 40 years.

Mrs. Reid had a mother's touch in the classroom, and she drew her students in with her warm smile and amazing personality. Betty Reid made you feel important. She made you feel like you mattered, and she took an active interest in all of her students. I never forget the way she mothered me and made me feel like, even though she had other children to teach, that I was one of her favorites. It made me feel that no matter the damage that Frank was doing, she was going to do whatever she could to give me a safe haven for a few hours a day. Furthermore, she made me feel like I was a good boy under her watch. It's been 40 years, but I have never forgotten one teacher's heart and her loving and caring ways. They say special people touch you in a special way, and I am eternally grateful for the impact Mrs. Reid had on my life. This woman was, without a doubt, a difference maker in my life. She chose to do so much more than just fulfill her job description. Mrs. Reid was always there with a kind word, a smile, a hug, or a pat on the back that seemed to say, "You are doing great and I'm proud of you."

There are countless great teachers out there who try to make a difference every day in both big and small ways, and I applaud every one of you. I ask every teacher who is reading this book to please understand that you are making such a huge difference. You are more valuable to your students and others than you may ever really know or fully understand. I didn't tell Betty Reid all of my problems, but she knew I was hurting in some way and somehow, she was always able to help me feel better. I was a nice, likeable kid, but I wanted to be funny, and to be liked, and I didn't care whether my friends laughed with me or at me.

The only problem with my foolishness was that there were consequences for acting out. I was paddled quite a bit, and it was just my luck I was catching it on both ends – at home and at school. No one from school knew what was going on at my home, and if I deserved that paddle they were going to they were going to give me the wallops I had coming to me. The thing I dreaded most was the school calling home about my bad behavior. This was my worst nightmare, because it was double jeopardy for yours truly. Frank would be standing in the doorway with a belt, growling, "Get your ass in here boy, you are going to get it." I found a way to withstand those beatings; I knew as long as he wasn't punching me or pinning me to the ground I could deal with the belt.

I am now 52 years old, and it might surprise you that a teacher from fourth grade, one that I had in class over 40 years ago, stood out from all the rest and made such a difference. I certainly had plenty of nice teachers along the way, but Betty Reid stood out to me then, as she does so to this day. She cared enough to do all she could to help a young broken fourth-grader feel a shred of dignity and feel loved.

Teachers do an excellent job every day, but if you are a teacher I urge you to please channel your inner Betty Reid and never forget you are so much more than a teacher. You have the potential to be a difference-maker and even a life changer for a frightened, belittled child like me. You may very well be the only positive influence in an abused child's life.

Betty Reid was all of that and more to me, and I am beyond grateful to her for stepping in to help me when I needed it the most. She didn't have to care, she didn't have to go the extra mile, and she didn't have to make it a point to help me but I thank God that she did. She left an indelible mark on me that I have never forgotten. The greatest lessons she taught me are compassion, love, caring, and understanding for others no matter what they are going through. Betty Reid came into my life when I was in desperate need to be treated with kindness. If you ever think for one minute that teachers don't make a difference, I ask you to think again. Teachers impact students every day in ways both seen and unseen. I am living proof. To all of the teachers who give their best every day please know you are making a huge impact on the lives of so many others... even when you may not even know it.

## 12  Teachers Make a Difference, Part 2: Lois Campbell Simms

*Nothing is Impossible, the word itself says I'm Possible.*
  *-Audrey Hepburn*

When I was a senior in high school, I started my career in broadcasting doing daily reports from my high school through DECA (Distributive Education Clubs of America, Incorporated). My teacher, Lois Campbell (now Lois Simms) was a wonderful woman – very smart, spunky and full of energy. She introduced me to broadcasting because she felt it may be a great fit for me, and in so doing she changed my life. She took an interest in me, and I always felt that she truly cared for my fellow classmates and me. She always went above and beyond her job description, and I know she could sense that I was like a ship at sea floating with no direction. She was like a rescue ship, helping me find the way to go.

At that time I had no career path, no earthly idea what I was going to do with my future, and she gave me the tools to turn my love for sports into a legitimate career path. It meant the world to me that she took the time to help me find direction, and I will always owe her a debt of gratitude. Thanks to Mrs. Simms' caring and leadership, as a senior I was named high school broadcaster of the year (1983) for reporting the news at North Stafford High School.

## 13   A Larger Than Life Impact: Thomas Tate

*It's not whether you get knocked down, it's whether you get back up.*
   *-Vince Lombardi*

Thomas Tate was a larger-than life African-American police officer who bonded with a white quarterback from the country. Tom always let me know that he had my back and that he cared for me as a person. He taught me a lot about looking at the content of one's character not just the outer shell of a person. He was someone I could talk to, and even though I never went deep into my problems I knew he understood where I had come from and some of what I had dealt with.

Tom told me on many occasions about the dangers of his job as a police officer. He would say, "If trouble comes and I'm called into a gun battle situation, my feeling is, I'd rather be tried by 12 than carried by 8." He would further make statements like, "Jamie, you have to understand, I love my family and I am going home to see them every night, so if it comes down to me or the bad guy there is no decision to be made." He looked at me with all the seriousness in the world, and I knew he was not joking.

Tragically and unbelievably my friend Tom, a man who was seemingly made of steel, died at home in his own garage changing the universal joint in his car when it rolled down on him and killed him. I cried my eyes out at the loss of this beloved coach, friend, and mentor. I used to always think about it and wish that one of my teammates or I could have been there to help him in his garage that day, to have a chance to save him and come through for him as he had always done for us. Tom's accident was stupefying to me on every level. Anyone who knew Tom Tate would use descriptive words like rock solid, indestructible, and hero for laying his life on the line for the citizens of Prince William County.

# A Game Ball for Frank

I spoke at his funeral, and it was an extremely sad day that left me with a huge feeling of emptiness. It was a major loss on so many levels; he was just an irreplaceable person. He was more than a coach – he was my friend – and he had a long lasting impact on me which helped prepare me to lead my own team on its own amazing journey.

Tom Tate was an American original, and he is sorely missed by his family, friends and players. We loved Tom then as we do now, and I always felt he knew how much he meant to us all and he always let us know that he had our backs. He always told me that I could do anything and urged me to never accept mediocrity. Anyone who knew Tom Tate could not help but be positively influenced by him. I was blessed to have him be such a guiding force in my life.

Years later, as my team marched towards a national championship many never knew that Tom Tate was there for the ride, and I felt that he was with us through our magical season. His leadership helped forge me into the coach I was, and I thank him for rooting for the Generals from his heavenly perch. I know that he's proud of me, and I'll forever be grateful for the impact he had on me as both a player and as a coach. I know you may wonder, "How do you know or feel something that you can't explain?" but it happened game after game after game. It was a feeling of a presence that I couldn't explain if I tried. Tom Tate may have had a hand in a few fumbles and interceptions and I had no doubt he was watching me from above. When the scoreboard would light up like a pinball machine and we would shut people down defensively, I could hear him saying something like, "You see that kid down there? He's doing great, and that team plays hard just like I used to coach them to." His booming voice was never far from my mind, and I would think of it whenever we needed a big play or a big stop on defense. I would not have had half the success were it not for the examples he set for me and my teammates.

During your life people come in, and some you never forget, I thank the unforgettable Tom Tate for his impact on my life and the lives of everyone he ever came in contact with. We are all better for having known Tom.

## 14   The Power of a Best Friend: Steve Carey

*Set your goals high and don't stop until you get there*
*-Bo Jackson*

Steven Scott Carey is my childhood best friend and remains so to this day. We grew up several blocks away from each other and attended the same elementary school – Triangle Elementary School. We eventually both moved from Triangle to Stafford, VA, around the same time, and we have lived near each other for over 40 years. As a matter of fact, as adults we live just a couple of miles away from each other. When we were young, we hit it off immediately for several reasons. We both loved our mothers deeply, neither of us had fathers in our lives, and we both had siblings suffering from a form of disability. They say people are put in your life for a purpose, and I have no doubt that Steve and I helped each other through things that only we understood, forging a bond will never be broken.

Steve is currently a captain in the Stafford Sheriff's Department in Stafford, VA, and I could not be prouder of him and what he has accomplished. The only thing more powerful than Steve's physical strength is the strength of his heart. He has always been one of the strongest men I know; he once bench-pressed over 600 pounds. But more importantly, he has a huge heart and has always had a penchant for helping others any chance he can. One time he put on a power-lifting show with a group of weightlifters to raise money for a young man in need of an organ transplant, and I witnessed him bench-press 315 pounds 39 times. Another time, when the two of us were lifting weights at a gym, he asked me to spot him on a lift of over 600 pounds. I half-jokingly said to him that if something went wrong, I would not be able to move that weight and I would be calling 911 for help. Fortunately for both us, we never needed to make that emergency call.

Every time I needed someone, in my hardest moments, Steve has been there to support and encourage me. I have always been able to tell him anything, confident that he will listen. But even though I never doubted that he would help me carry any burden, there were times when I withheld details about my trials from Steve, because I needed to laugh and escape my reality, and I was afraid talking about it would ruin our fun. If there was a Hall of Fame for great human beings who make a difference in the lives of others, Steve would be in on the first ballot.

There are no words to adequately describe my feelings for Steve and the impact he has had on my life. I know that he knows that I would be there for him 24 hours a day seven days a week and that there is nothing I wouldn't do for him. During the worst parts of Frank's abuse, when it was a living hell, time with Steve was my one true escape. I had a friend who loved and accepted me despite how terrible things were at home, and that fact allowed me to forget my own personal war zone for just a little while.

Steve lived in a tiny area of Stafford County called Widewater, VA. He lived with his mother, Joyce Ann Carey, who was one of the most wonderful women I had ever met in my life. She was a big woman, and her size was only outmatched by her heart. She worked at the local gas station and she was also a volunteer fire fighter for the Widewater Rescue Squad. In her earlier days, she developed a reputation for maintaining law and order while working at a restaurant and bar called the Mid-Way Diner. Legend has it that when customers had one drink too many, she wouldn't hesitate to toss them out the door. She was a single mother, raising a big family. She had four daughters – Diane, Barbara Ann, Theresa (otherwise known as Peanut), and Cindy.

There is no doubt that she loved her daughters, but I always felt her pride and joy was her son. Steve had a nickname, Charlie Brown, which was given to him by his father because he was bald as a baby and which folks in Widewater still use to this day. Steve used to joke that his father never gave him anything but that nickname. Joyce, on the other hand, never stopped giving. She was an amazing woman who was committed to helping kids. She was a very giving woman who never saw color, and she helped feed and clothe many friends of ours who were African-American. She was a shining example of how to treat people with dignity and respect at all times.

Despite lacking a college degree, Joyce taught me the true meaning of carrying yourself with pride and professionalism at all times. Joyce Carey, in many ways, showed her caring heart to everyone that she came in contact with. I considered her my second mother, and I loved her for caring about me as she did. When things were rough with Frank, I found myself wishing I could live with Steve, and we often talked about that possibility, staying up late and talking about the important issues of the day, like sports and girls and sports and girls. I know the way Joyce dealt with people helped mold Steve into the leader he has become as a man. Steve dealt with his sister's disability, and I dealt with my brother who had his own disability.

I met Steve's dad only one time, and I always felt that his dad missed out on one of the nicest, most wonderful people on earth. Steve had it all: blondish-brownish hair, blue eyes, handsome, the Homecoming King, a stellar athlete and he was respected and admired by his peers and liked by everyone. His dad missed out on a once-in-a-lifetime son that anyone would have been proud to have raised. We were so close that our head football coach Jimmy Null once asked me, "Where is your shadow?" Steve and I both came from nothing; we weren't wealthy or privileged, and we weren't about to let our lack of material possessions bother us. We knew we weren't rich, but we did the very best we could with everything we had. Joyce was a single mom, and he was the man of the house from very early on. I loved hanging out at his house because there was no man there – there was no Frank or Frank-like presence.

Steve lived in a doublewide trailer in a small country area where everyone knew everyone, and he was known simply as Charlie Brown from Widewater. I would always ask him what he would do in certain situations to gauge what I should do, and he always gave great advice. We made a pact when we were little that remains to this day. We both promised each other that we would never, under any circumstances, try drugs of any kind. That is something that we are both very proud of, that we have both lived our lives drug-free. Because of our siblings with disabilities, we have both been reminded repeatedly how fortunate we were. Steve has never been judgmental, and he has always remained one hundred percent supportive of our friendship and me. I give Steve a great deal of credit for helping me stay on the straight and narrow, and I feel I did the same for him in return.

Can one person truly make a difference? Without question, Steve made my life better in so many ways, both seen and unseen, and I am truly grateful. Steve Carey personifies the word friend in every way and it's apparent to me that God had a hand in bringing us together. It has been amazing to see the parallels that our lives have taken. I am very proud to have been able to maintain a lasting friendship that has withstood the test of time. Steve is the strongest person I have ever known physically, but his greatest strength is found in his character, his integrity, and his love for his wife Cheryl and his two daughters Kendall and Kelsey, as well as his extended family and friends.

Steve Carey has my never-ending friendship, love, and support, and I thank him for being there at times when no one else was. He never turned his back on me, he never gave up on me and he has always been there with unwavering support through my darkest days. He has rooted for my success as I have for his. I know that I didn't have much going for me growing up, but to take a line from Steve's favorite movie "It's A Wonderful Life", I have always felt like the richest man in town for having had Steve Carey in my life and being able to call him my best friend.

## 15   Small Things That Come Back in Big Ways

*The only place where success comes before work is in the dictionary.*
   *-Vidal Sassoon*

**M**y mom always told me to treat people with respect, and she always told me that if you treat people well and do kind things it will invariably come back to you in ways big and small, sometimes when you least expect it. I have tried to live my life in this way, which was given to me by the one source that always knows best, Mom.

When the Fredericksburg Generals first started I was struggling financially, as my last name was definitely not Rockefeller. In order to build the type of team I envisioned, I knew I would have to do certain things. I wanted to take as much weight off the players as possible so that they could focus on winning and carrying out the game plans to perfection. We were able to secure a team chiropractor, a team dentist, and a team trainer, and we had meals provided on game day by the Old Country Buffet. We needed uniforms, helmets, transportation, a home field and locker rooms, so we had more needs out of the gate than you can imagine.

As the old Jerry Reed hit song went, "We had a long way to go and a short time to get there." I was recruiting the best of the best, and with that you want to offer the players best that you possibly can. We had postgame celebrations at a local bar called The Golden Rail, we did my coaches show from Damon's, but we needed help in a big way. Getting back to Mom's golden rule about the way good things sometimes come back around, things were about to take a major turn for the better.

I was traveling down Interstate 95 one day when I noticed a family with a truck pulling a small camper behind it. I was about to get off the next exit to go home when I noticed the back left tire had caught on fire and there was a chance the whole camper could go up in flames. I pulled up ahead and slowed them down, urging them to pull over, and fortunately they did. I ran up to the cab, where the husband and wife were sitting with the three kids in the back truck seat. I said, "Sir, your camper's tire is on fire and we need to put the fire out." I had some towels and we smothered it. There was a strong smell of burnt rubber in the air. The camper somehow didn't burn, but the flames had made their mark on the sidewall of the camper so it was close to becoming worse than it turned out.

We waited until things cooled off, and then we changed his tire with the spare. I shook his hand and he pulled his wallet out and he asked, "How much do I owe you?" I said, "You don't owe me anything buddy, have a great trip through Virginia and I hope your family has a great vacation." The family waved, I waved back and I felt like I had made a few friends and had helped them on the way to their destination. I felt great about what happened and thought about a family vacation that could have been ruined, but fortunately it all turned out for the best.

The next afternoon, I was looking for sponsors for our football team and I stopped into a Checkers Hamburgers location that was just getting ready to open in Fredericksburg. I spoke with the person who was overseeing the building at the time and I asked if I could speak to the owner about sponsoring us. The person said, "Can you come back at 6 p.m.? The owner is Mr. Walter Dorsey and he would be happy to speak with you, as he is a big sports fan."

I went home, made some calls and headed back to meet Mr. Dorsey, who could not have been nicer. He told me about his son John, who had played football at Connecticut and was a fourth-round selection of the Green Bay Packers. John had a very successful career with the Packers, and his 35 tackles with the Packers as a special teams player in 1984 is still a team record. John worked his way up through the Packers organization, as a scout, then as the director of college scouting, then as the Seattle Seahawks' director of player personnel. John Dorsey is now the general manager of the Kansas City Chiefs.

He has always been a friend to me and he is one of the best people in all of professional sports.

His father, Walter, was great to me and the Generals owe him a tremendous debt of gratitude for all he did for our football team. He wrote me a five-figure check that paid for our team's uniforms, a large part of the player's helmets and equipment, transportation and things like game tape, locker room rentals and footballs. He said he wanted to also give each of the players a Checkers card for a free Checkers hamburger every week, and he also did other things for them after victories. He was one of the nicest people I had ever met, and he was a difference maker.

With Checkers and Walter Dorsey on our side, we were ready to go out and make businessmen like him and Fredericksburg proud to support this team. I drove home thinking of Mom, and how the lesson of doing good to others and seeing it come back around had worked out just like she said it would. It was a great moment of serendipity and I was not going to question it; we received the sponsor we had been searching for.

I also want to single out two Checkers employees, who were always great to us, and who always treated us in a first class way. Barry Loescher and Larry Harvey were two of the store's managers, and they are two of the best people we have ever worked with. They both represent the brand with class, and they are two of the reasons that Checkers has enjoyed huge success locally, regionally, and nationally. They are great leaders, and we thank them both for being such tremendous partners and supporters of our team. Checkers and Walter Dorsey set the Generals on a direct path to a championship; we went from being in a desperate need to a team with a bright future because of a football fan and a business owner who wanted us to succeed

That's just one example but here is another prime example of my mom's life lessons coming back to me in a big way, I had worked through the years in broadcasting with my great friend, Mike Neville, and many years ago we worked at 96 Rock located at the time in Ladysmith, VA. A super-nice guy named Walden Abernathy, who also owned the Ladysmith Pharmacy, owned the station. During our time at the station, there were a couple of young guys that used to hang out together, and who both had a love of broadcasting. One was the station owner's son, Greg Abernathy, and his close friend, Mitchell Bradley. They were kids, who had fun and cut up, and did things normal teenagers do. We treated them with respect and were always nice to them as Mike and I had once been young reporters trying to break into the business. It hadn't been easy by a long shot, so we always tried to look out for others whenever we could.

Last year, I was inquiring about jobs at some different radio stations. When I called one, the voice on the other end was very friendly and sounded somewhat familiar. It was none other than Mitchell Bradley. That teenage kid that once ran around with his buddy while we did our show was now in charge of bringing new shows and new talent on board. My mind immediately flashed to what Mom always said, and he told me he remembered how nice Mike and I were to him. If you want to talk about a classic case of why you should always treat everyone you come in contact with respect, it's because you never really know what may happen at any point in the future. I had no clue that the 16-year-old kid that I once showed kindness to would, 17 years later, be in a position to bring me on board and be my boss at ESPN Radio.

I am very fortunate to work with a great team of people, from Mitchell to our outstanding general manager Buck Albritton, to my excellent producer Andrew Wallace; they are all great to work with. Andrew is a multitalented young man with a very bright future. Andrew has done a lot of great things with my show, "The Sports King," and working with him has been great from day one. I am fortunate to be part of a great local sports lineup that features "Sports Phone with Big Al", hosted by Al Coleman and "Hardly

Workin'" with Greg Burton and his great producer Matt Josephs, who is known to many as mid-major Matt Josephs for his amazing knowledge of mid-major conference sports.

I know there are people that only treat others well if they think the other person can help them, which is foolhardy at best. I've always subscribed to the thinking of, "Be kind to everyone and treat everyone with respect, because you never know." I'm living proof that you should always be kind and treat people well, and I guarantee you at some juncture something will happen for you. Let me be clear, it may not always happen in your timeframe, but in some way, big or small, it will come back to you in a form of a blessing.

Here is one final example of how amazing things happen if you maintain a belief that anything is possible if you keep a positive attitude, regarding my sponsorship deal with Leesa Mattress. I had a meeting with Leesa CEO David Wolfe in Virginia Beach, VA to see if he would like to become the official studio-naming rights holder and the title sponsor of my radio show on ESPN 950 & Sports FM 100.5. During my nearly three-hour drive, I considered how a successful meeting would help my show, as well as the station. I spoke with God on the way down, and he listened, and then I doubled down and spoke to my Mom who had passed away in 2014. I am someone who believes in signs from above, and I asked my Mom specifically to look out for me, to help me put my best foot forward during the meeting. I wanted her to guide me and to watch over the meeting, and I told her that if she could bring me any luck I would be so grateful.

I pulled into the parking lot, which had more than 100 spaces, and there were only about 30 cars scattered throughout the parking lot. I texted Mr. Wolfe asking him where should I park, and he replied that he would get right back to me with the space number. Then he texted the number for the space that he wanted me to park in, which was number 21. The number 21 just happened to be my Mom's birthday, which is April 21st and it's a very lucky number for me. So you can think whatever you like, but for me, there is no one in the world that can convince me that my mom wasn't sending me a message. I got out of the car and walked to the back of the vehicle with a huge smile on my face and I took a photo of the No. 21. I looked at the number almost in tears and said, "Thank you Mom," knowing full well she was listening. I walked with a greater confidence, a greater sense of purpose. She sent me a clear message –"I'll be with you, you've got this, now go knock their socks off and get a deal done."

I was impressed with Leesa CEO David Wolfe from the moment I met him; he's one of those people who just makes things happen. He's a doer, and like all great businessmen he has extraordinary vision. As the meeting went on, I was meeting more and more people while David was on some high-level calls. He instructed his staff to show me around and he allowed me to meet everyone and see their offices.

I was called in to meet with David, and I found that David was not only a visionary, he was easy to talk to and he had a passion for sports. We talked sports, we talked business, and he agreed to become the naming rights holder for the studio as well as sponsor my nightly sports show. He signed a contract on the spot, shook my hand and told me how excited he was to work with me, and we have had the best time working together. He even hosts regular segments about soccer, his favorite sport.

With the signed contract in hand, and a great day with a company that I believe will be the No. 1 mattress company in the world one day, I headed toward the parking lot. I kissed my hand, bent down and placed it on the No. 21, and said, "Thank you Mom." I got in the car, and as I started down the road I looked toward the blue sky up ahead and thanked God for his help and all he did to make this happen. My thoughts then turned to my mom and the power of 21. Some may think it was just happenstance but I know better; my Mom was there and she helped guide me that day and I KNEW the meeting would be a success.

I called David Wolfe days later to thank him and to tell him the story of what happened that day. I'll never forget meeting a one-of-a-kind business owner with a one-of-a-kind business and the major impact he made on me that day. This all happened with an incredible meeting that was already predestined to succeed thanks to my Mom encouraging me in her own indomitable way. I had no doubt that she would be with me the entire time, as she showed me from the moment that I stepped out of the car. Thanks to David, God, Mom, and the power of 21, that meeting – and the relationship that formed from it – was better than anything I could have ever imagined.

# Part 4 – Family and the Future

*Believe in yourself and all that you are, and know that there is something inside you that is greater than any obstacle*
    *-Christian D. Larson*

# A Game Ball for Frank

# 16  Hall of Fame Mother

*Happiness is not something readymade it comes from your own actions*
  *-Dalai Lama*

If there was a Hall of Fame for mothers my mom, June King, would be in on the first ballot. Growing up, she was my best friend on top of being my mom; she was someone who gave of herself in every way, and she has my never-ending respect, admiration, and love. Some may wonder if I carry any resentment or if I was mad at my Mom for what I went through, and the answer is unequivocally no. I certainly wish the events of my childhood with Frank had turned out differently, but my Mom was working and was not present during the majority of my battles with him. Frank was very careful about the timing of his attacks. When my Mom saw things out of line she instinctively jumped in, like a mother bear protecting her cub. It was when she was out of sight that things were at their absolute worst. Mom took up for me constantly, which only angered Frank more and made things unbearable. I went to great lengths to avoid upsetting my mom, because I loved her so much and wanted to protect her.

**Jamie and his Mom**

My Mom was born June Ernestine Donohoe on April 21, 1927. Born and raised in Washington D.C, she was an excellent track athlete and was ahead of her time in terms of her athletic ability. She met my father, Robert Livingston Richards, and they proceeded to have Steve, Brett, Earl, and me – the baby of the bunch. My dad left my mom when I was a baby and she had to raise us on our own for a while, and she eventually met and married Frank. I think she felt he would be a good provider, and she couldn't have dreamed how terrible his treatment of us would actually be. Frank obviously fell for my Mom, which I can understand, as she was beautiful and had a great personality as well. My Mom was always very easygoing, and she was never one who felt that she had to keep up with the Joneses. She always told us that we were capable of anything that we put our minds to, and she was right. Steve and Earl are two of the brightest academic minds you will ever find; Steve went on to become a mining engineer, and Earl works as an accountant.

My Mom would always say if you treated people right, and if you were a good person, you could go far in life. To Frank's credit, he was a good provider. We never went hungry and we had a roof over our heads. Frank and Mom would have horrible fights, a lot of them centered around something one of my brothers did. He was relentless, and to her credit, she would not back down. When she heard him tearing me down she would often interject into the conversation to take the heat off of me. Mom worked incredibly hard and always tried to do her best for all of us. Throughout my childhood, when angered, Frank would yell at me, "Go to bed. No dinner for you." On those nights I would lie in bed crying, my stomach growling, and Mom would always sneak me a sandwich or a drink. She crossed enemy lines to make sure I had something to eat. She was not going to let her son go to bed hungry and she always tried to get a snack to me at the very least.

My mom is the kind of mom who would give you her last quarter because she always put others first. She was caring, giving, and loving, and were it not for her, I honestly don't know if I would be here today. Her smile, friendship, and love meant more to me than anything. I speak for my brothers too when I say we were all so very fortunate to have had her in our lives. She worked so much when I was in school, but she did her best in later years to attend every Fredericksburg Generals game. I remember when I played quarterback at North Stafford High School in Garrisonville, VA, she only got to see me play once or twice. One of the times she was in the stands was also one of the rare occasions when I threw an interception, and I was dejected about it after. "Jay," she said, "you really throw the ball well; you throw a perfect spiral." I responded, "Mom, I threw it to the wrong team," and she said, "It was a beautiful pass no matter who caught it." A mother's love is sometimes blind, but always appreciated.

Years later, when I began coaching, I would always walk out on the field early with the specialists and the quarterbacks and spot her sitting in the parking lot. I would wave and she would honk to let me know she was there. She became a fixture sitting in her little red car, honking her horn and flicking her lights with every big play and every touchdown or field goal, and she loved every minute of it. Frank sat with her during this time; he had to because she was not going to miss me coaching, no matter what. She felt she needed to make it up to me because she missed so many of my games when I was younger. It was great to see her and even Frank there as she was cheering her son on as I navigated our team towards a national championship. My Mom has never turned her back on me and she has never been judgmental. I was proud that she was there every step of the way.

June King was my hero, my rock and the one person who was always there without fail. Her death was unquestionably the worst day of my life, and I am grateful that she had the chance to see her son win it all and achieve such an amazing goal. She also saw me grant Frank a level of forgiveness and take the high road before he passed away. June King passed away on April 11, 2014, just eleven days shy of her 87th birthday. Her loss was devastating to me on so many levels because for the longest time she was all I had. I loved her, and I take great solace in the fact that I know she knew that and that I know how much she loved me. I know I speak for all of my brothers when I say God blessed us all with a once-in-a-lifetime mother named June King.

## 17   Forever Terrific: Brett T

*There are no traffic jams along the extra mile*
  *-Roger Staubach*

On July 14, 1955 my mom gave birth to her second son, Brett Thomas Richards. I always affectionately called him Brett T. Brett was a beautiful child, and my mom always kept him dressed immaculately. As time went on, things started to go wrong and it was determined that Brett suffered from a form of brain damage from birth. If that wasn't bad enough, he also suffered with epileptic seizures throughout his life. It always saddened me, and it still does to this day, that Brett never had the opportunities or chances that I or my other brothers have had. I know it hurt my Mom deeply and she felt powerless about Brett's physical struggles. I can't begin to imagine the feelings of hurt and helplessness that parents of handicapped children can carry on their shoulders. I know some of those parents, like my mom, sometimes blame themselves. I saw my mom hurting about Brett, but I didn't know how to comfort her or ease her pain.

The agreement that was worked out during the divorce proceedings was that Brett would go with our father and live in Florida, where my dad could care for him. He was a child with special needs, and my mom had three other boys to raise at that time. I know this hurt her deeply; she never wanted to be separated from Brett and she never felt good about the arrangement. I only got to see Brett a couple times as a child, and we always laughed and played together. I never paid attention to what he couldn't do. I just knew he was my brother and I loved him no matter what.

Despite his handicap, Brett was able to do certain things that my father taught him to do. He helped my Dad hang siding on houses and learned how to do other manual labor. I saw his handwriting in later years, and I would compare it to that of a second grader. He did not go to a regular school, and opportunities were limited for him. He saw my father have to hotwire his old work truck to get it started so many times that he remembered how to do it exactly. I can't explain the wiring in his brain but I know that he could take a transistor radio apart and put it back together again but he could not differentiate between right and wrong.

Brett was the simplest and kindest person you ever met. He loved music, especially the Partridge Family from the hit TV show with the same name. He would listen to their music over and over and over again. He would always carry his radio boom box with him with his favorite tape collection in tow. One of his favorite television shows was *The Dukes of Hazzard*.

Inspired by that show, he always wanted to drive, but because of his epilepsy he was never supposed to get behind the wheel. After our dad passed away Brett moved to Virginia, and one day he asked me, "Jay, can you teach me how to drive, please?" It broke my heart, and I had to leave the room to compose myself because I was getting very emotional. How could I tell him that I wouldn't be able to teach him? I hated not being able to do things for him, and I hated telling him no. Although I offered to take him anywhere anytime, he was determined to drive. This man who would never harm a soul was arrested many times for the same thing – taking a car or a truck for a drive. He never meant to harm anyone, but he wanted to drive more than anything, and being told no was not a deterrent. He never felt he was doing anything wrong, because he wanted to drive a car so badly.

With his background and medical history, Brett should never have been incarcerated, but should have instead been placed in a halfway house or someplace with proper supervision. He was considered a "tweener," a functioning adult with the mentality of a grade-schooler, which meant they had no place at the time to care for someone like him. Time and time again he would get released and go straight out to find a car and take a drive. He would drive for a while, run out of gas, and walk until he saw another unattended car. If it was an older car, he could hotwire it, and if it wasn't he kept walking until he found a car with the keys in it that he could take for another driving adventure.

Brett didn't care what he drove; he just wanted to drive. One night he found an old parked school bus, and he climbed aboard for a late-night bus ride. He always did the same thing -- he would drive as far as he could until the vehicle ran out of gas, and then he would pull over, park the car and get out. To him, it was just about wanting an experience. When Brett wasn't in trouble because of his driving situation he would stay with us, and Mom doted on him, which I always felt was her way of trying to catch up for the lost time she regretted. She would take him places and they would go to lunch and do special things, which made both of them happy. Parking and watching fireworks, going out to eat, running errands or feeding the ducks, they were two peas in a pod.

I had a favorite nickname for Brett, and it was a little ritual we shared. Every time I saw Brett, day or night, I would always say hello or just blurt out, "Brett T!" and I always ended that by saying, "and the T stands for.." and he would always say with enthusiasm and a smile on his face, "TERRIFIC!" We did this every single time we saw each other without fail, and it made both of us smile.

I carry Brett with me, especially when I give talks, because no matter how bad I had it, no matter what I had to endure, Brett had it worse. He was my shining example of a person who did his best to look at the good in everyone and find joy in every day, despite the setbacks. No matter what goes wrong, I always have Brett in the back of my mind as a reminder of how to battle every day no matter the odds.

When Brett was in his early forties, he started going to the doctor complaining of stomach pain, and he was in and out of hospitals quite a bit. He was part of a club in Fredericksburg, VA, called the Kenmore Club, which is a club designed to help people who have mental and physical challenges. Brett was well-liked by everyone in the club, and he even had a girlfriend named Diane, and I was thrilled that he had a woman that he loved and cared for in his life.

Unfortunately, the good times would not last for Brett as his health problems worsened. I remember visiting him in the hospital and he had a tube running from his throat down to a bag on his side. When he drank orange juice it just wet his throat, but the orange juice was not getting processed through his body and his body began to slowly shut down. Although he knew he was sick, I don't think he knew how sick he truly was. Brett was suffering from colorectal cancer, and he was losing the battle

One of my big brothers, someone I had always admired for his courage and fighting spirit, was dying, and as I watched it unfold my heart was breaking piece by piece. It was another devastating blow for me, and my mom was hurting so deeply that I didn't know what to say or do. I was totally helpless on every level, and I didn't know if I would ever be the same after watching Brett succumb to this terrible disease.

Mom went downstairs to the cafeteria one day during Brett's last week, and I was holding his hand. I asked Brett if he wanted me to write Mom a letter telling her how he felt about her. He said, "Sure Jay," and I said, "OK, what do you want to say?" He said, "Tell Mom I love her very much." I was covering my face so he could not see me crying as I wrote this beautiful gesture of love for the woman he loved more than anything in the world. They were not only mother and son, they were also great friends, and she never treated him any different than the rest of us. I saw strength in my Mom through the way she treated everyone with love and dignity, and it made my love and respect for her only grow.

I was with my mom in Brett's room on Oct. 5, 2000 when my big brother passed away at the much-too-young age of 45. It devastated me beyond words and caused me a tremendous amount of pain to see the battle he fought against a cancer he didn't fully understand. To me it was the cruelest thing that could happen to someone who had experienced a lifetime of unfortunate obstacles and medical issues. Brett was brave, and he will always be a hero for all of the hardships he endured, but through it all he never, ever complained and he carried himself like a champion every day until the end.

It's truly unbearable watching someone you love more than anything take his last breath while you are unable to do anything to help. It has to be the single most excruciating pain of loss I had ever felt at that time in my life, and I wouldn't wish that pain on anyone. In his last few hours, we were able to talk a little bit, and I kissed his forehead and tried to offer any comfort I could. I kept telling him over and over how much we loved him and how much I loved him. "I love you too Jay," he said, "I know buddy" and I told him God loved him and was with him and would be with him always. In his final moments I held his hand and rubbed his head, sobbing uncontrollably as he looked so peaceful. I whispered, "Brett T, I love you so much. I love you so much. You are terrific. You are so terrific. I love you."

Brett T was the most terrific brother anyone could ever ask for. Brett passed away as we were holding him, while reassuring him of our love and God's love, and there is no doubt that I appreciate life and all of the people in my life more because God chose to make Brett my brother.

I ask anyone who is approaching 50 years of age to please get a colonoscopy, because it could very well save your life. If you have a family history, please get seen sooner. In most cases, colon cancer is a treatable cancer when it's detected early enough, and I would be doing a terrible disservice to Brett's memory if I didn't urge you to be proactive and get a colonoscopy. I am happy to announce that I was proactive and I was blessed to receive great news from the doctor that everything was all clear. The first thought I had, upon hearing the news, was that I wish Brett would have received the same news and that things would have somehow changed before it was too late.

Brett is gone, but he will never be forgotten. I hope every person that reads this story will call and make an appointment to go get a colonoscopy as soon as possible. If anyone decides to get tested because of reading this chapter on Brett T. and becomes inspired to go get the colonoscopy procedure, then they definitely owe Brett T. a debt of gratitude. My brother Brett is now helping people that he never met through his story, as he is making a huge difference in the lives of others. I for one happen to think that is incredibly terrific in every way!

## 18   More Brotherly Love: Steve, Earl, and Kelly

*If you can dream it you can achieve it*
*   -Zig Ziglar*

My brothers are all unique and very talented. We are all different in our interests and talents. Yet, each has both supported and inspired me.

### The Eagle-Eye: Steve

When I think of Steve, I think of his amazing hand eye coordination, which allows him to excel in many sports. He is an avid shooter dating back to his youth, where he was a clay pigeon-shooting prodigy. He excelled in track, and was an excellent triple jumper. He became a great billiards player. While attending Virginia Tech (and becoming a huge Hokies fan), Steve earned a Mining Engineering degree. As an undergraduate, he put his prodigious billiards skill to good use, teaching the sport to the students of Radford University, then a women's' college. He was popular with his female students, eventually meeting his future wife Peggy.

Today, Steve travels the world for Carlson Software, selling mining software and training engineers to use it. He and his wife Peggy live in Maysville, Kentucky. Steve was an Eagle Scout and is still active in Boy Scouting. He loves to golf, travel and shoot guns in his free time and he is very involved with his church.

# A Game Ball for Frank

### *A Self-Taught Genius: Earl*

I am constantly amazed by all of the things Earl has done through-out his life – by teaching himself. Earl is a self-taught musician who can play a variety of instruments including rhythm guitar and key-boards. As a teen, he taught himself how to work on cars, which he continues to take cars apart and put them back together very quickly. This is handy, because he now owns a race car. He has a tremendous memory and is one of the brightest people you will ever meet. He always excelled in anything academic related. He recently earned his CPA Certification after passing the exam and may one day own an accounting firm.

Earl resides in Fredericksburg, VA and is currently an accountant for The Phillips Collection, an art Museum based in Washington, D.C. It is hardly surprising that in his spare time he plays in a band and races in the Sports Car Club of America. He is a very good golfer and he is a frequent concert goer as well. He is one of the nicest people you will ever meet and he is universally liked by eve-ryone he meets.

### *A Hands-on Expert: Kelly*

My kid brother Kelly inherited his father Frank's ability to create beauty with his hands, and his mother's determination to build a great life for those around him. He has a passion for home improve-ment and he is great at it. I call him the "Ty Pennington" of the fam-ily, as he reminds me of the host of the show *Extreme Home Makeover*. Kelly can fix anything, he can build anything and he is at his best when he is building or developing something. Kelly is an extremely hard worker. He works daily building decks, finishing basements and anything using his hands he excels at. He frames houses, re-places carpet; anything that can beautify any home.

Like Earl, Kelly is a Motorsports fan. He loves to follow NASCAR in a big way. In work and in play, he is someone who puts maxi-mum effort into anything he takes on. He currently works in the construction industry and he resides in Spotsylvania, VA.

# 19 My Life Now and into the Future, Generally Speaking

*I've got a theory that if you give 100% all of the time, somehow things will work out in the end*
*-Larry Bird*

This book was 20 years in the making, and it began as a cathartic way for me to deal with something I couldn't talk about. It has helped this "broken" individual deal with "unfinished business" as my friend, Thomas Dozier, put it. This was a story of love, retribution, second chances, and redemption, and above all it showed the hearts of champions that each and every one of my coaches and players had. We were all broken in ways, some more than others.

Leadership of this team gave me the one thing I had always wanted – the opportunity to be considered a good person who could do something great, no matter how much I was told I wouldn't or couldn't. It's also the story of a 47-year-old NFL kicker, well past his prime, with a failed marriage and a business that was going under, who needed to be part of something special. Mark Moseley needed to know that he could turn his life around, and he was also in search of one last exclamation point on an illustrious career. The one constant that stood above all else is our love for each other and how much we needed each other.

Think about it: if we went 3-7, I would have never gotten close to redemption. I would have been a failure in Frank's eyes and in the eyes of my coaching staff, players, fans, sponsors and everyone associated with the program, and it would have been devastating on so many levels. There was an enormous amount of pressure on me, but I would not let the possibility of failure enter into my mind. In fact, it was the fear of failure that relentlessly drove me to success. I like to take a quote from a movie I love, *Apollo 13*, "Failure is not an option." The thing that no one realized but me was that in order to expel my demons, I had to build a champion.

It's not always X's and O's; in football often it's the Johnny's and Joe's. In the case of the Generals great talent, combined with very good game planning, can make a coach look great. I out recruited everyone, working tirelessly to get the best players on the field. I knew that if I was able to get them there and if we had a solid game plan then we would reach our destination. For me, I owe the greatest debt of gratitude to the players that made this dream happen – the players who bought into the recruiting pitch, the game plans and the vision. They are my heroes, and they are all champions. My story, and my quest to heal, would have been impossible if those men didn't execute and deliver game after game after game. I loved those guys then, as I do now, and it's because of them that I achieved my lifelong goal.

Today I'm doing what I love, talking sports five nights a week on ESPN 950 in Richmond, VA. The station has set me up with a home studio, so I can do the show at home or at the station's studio. I am the proud father of two children that I love so very much, Jennie and Patrick. Jennie, the oldest, is an excellent athlete, playing soccer and field hockey in high school and earning a degree from Virginia Tech in Hospitality Tourism Management.

Patrick starred as a punter/kicker in high school at Spotsylvania High School for Coach Tim Coleman, where he won a State Championship in 1997, and later DeMatha High School in Hyattsville, MD, where he played for the legendary coach Bill McGregor. I am fortunate that Bill McGregor has become one of my closest friends and he has offered me great advice. He is a first class individual and in many people's opinion including mine he will go down as the greatest high school football coach of all time. Patrick was rated as one of the top high school kickers/punters in the nation in 2000. Patrick was also selected to the "George Michael Golden 11" as the top player in the entire Maryland, Virginia and D.C. area at his position and the highlight of Patrick's career, shown over and over on television, was an 83-yard punt out of the back of the end zone in the WCAC Championship game at RFK Stadium, the former home of the Washington Redskins. He had more than 30 college offers and decided to play for Ron Turner, brother to NFL coach Norv Turner, at the University of Illinois. He is currently in the United States Navy stationed in Norfolk, VA, serving proudly on the USS Lincoln.

I am also the grandfather to three of the best grandchildren you could ever ask for. Ryan, the oldest, actually won the MVP Award in basketball at Spotsylvania Middle School during his eighth grade year. The Dallas Mavericks' Justin Anderson, who went on to star at the University of Virginia, previously won the award.

Justin came on my radio show and he gave a shout out to Ryan, proving that he is a super-nice young man as well as a budding NBA superstar. I have been able to get to know his brother Edward, who is a wonderful young man who works closely with his brother and he does an excellent job for him. I jokingly told him that we have a plan to have Ryan grow to 6-foot-8, play for the Cavaliers and then get drafted by Mark Cuban and the Dallas Mavericks. Ryan is an excellent student and a great soccer and basketball player, but more importantly he is an outstanding young man.

My granddaughter Jillian is a rising sixth grader – an amazing young lady who is smart, pretty and the spitting image of her mom. She is active in the arts and she is very talented.

Then, there is my five-year-old grandson, Nathan. My wife says about Nathan, "There's your linebacker." He recently told us that he loves hockey, and when we asked him why he said, "Because you get to push people down." He loves the physical side of sports, and he hasn't really even started playing yet.

Last, but not least, is my wife, Denise, who has been with me since Nov. 10, 1992, the day after my 28th birthday. It was a Tuesday night and we saw "Passenger 57" with Wesley Snipes, and we have been together ever since. It's hard to put into words how much she has meant to me. Dating and being married to a football coach is not easy.

She has taken tickets, fed players on occasion, and ran concessions. She was always there to support the team and me in every way possible. I love her for believing in me and understanding that I was a broken person trying to become whole. She didn't understand why, and I didn't divulge a lot at first. Not because I didn't want her to

**Denise and Jamie**

know; I wanted to deal with it on my own and try to fix it on my own. I love her so much, and she helped me immensely in numerous ways. We couldn't have won a championship unless we had someone running the operational side of things, and she did a magnificent job at that. She means everything to me, and I can't thank her enough for all she did for the Generals and me. Few people ever knew this, but our owner Hal James had sold all of his stock in the team to Denise, making her the owner of the team. Talk about pressure! I had to win the championship, because I was living with the owner *and* the person who made sure the team operations ran smoothly.

I'm on the air nightly now. My producer Andrew Wallace and I put together a fun fast-paced program featuring some of the top names in sports and entertainment. We are very proud of that, and the show is doing very well. My hope is that we get syndicated, and if you know me, you know I'm driven and I want to be number one in all that I do, so I won't stop until we reach the top.

I am thankful for the accolades that came with winning the National Championship. Immediately after the season, then-President Clinton and First Lady Hillary Rodham Clinton sent me a signed picture with a note congratulating me on the accomplishment.

# A Game Ball for Frank

In one of the greatest honors of my life, I was recently contacted by Former San Francisco 49ers head coach, Hall of Fame linebacker, and Chicago Bears legend Mike Singletary about potentially working with him in a coaching capacity in the future. To receive a call, and a request, to possibly work with one of the greatest players to have ever played the game was, in a word, amazing. Singletary was a key part of what was arguably the most dominant NFL defensive team of all time—the 1985 Chicago Bears. I have so much respect for Mike Singletary, for the way he coaches, and how he lives his life. He is a man of faith and a great leader of men, and he deserves another chance to be a head coach, either in the NFL or for a major NCAA Division I college football program. I hope he gets the opportunity, because I have no doubt that he will win another championship if given the opportunity.

Would I do it, would I get back into coaching? There is only one opportunity that I would consider, and it would be to work with and for Mike Singletary. So if my phone rings and he asks me to join him I would be honored to do so. I have the confidence that I can win at any level. If I had an owner that gave me the latitude to pick my own coaches and have a great staff, then the optimist in me says I can bring home a winner. I have always considered myself a players' coach. I can recruit players because I love people and I know how to win. Like anything else in life, you have to have a game plan for success and then you have to follow it through.

Once again I must thank the Generals players, coaches and staff, because without them I would have never been in position to have such an amazing opportunity.

For the immediate future, my focus is on my wife Denise, our kids and grandkids, my radio show, and my puppy Holly and our newest puppy Callie. I've put some of my biggest broken pieces back together, and while I wonder if I'll ever be completely whole I'm proud of what I've achieved individually and what we accomplished as a team.

I'm not sure I'll ever stop asking questions like, "Why me?" and "What if was born to a father who cared and who treated me as a person who actually mattered?" But I've learned over time that I can't keep looking back. I have gained a measure of closure from my pain, and I finally feel like a person who can be proud of himself.

In the final analysis, back then I just wanted to be seen as a good boy, and then a good young man and then a good man. It was all I ever hoped for, and yet it wasn't meant to be in my early years. Now all of that has happened, and so I can have peace knowing that I really was a good boy and a good young man, and that now I'm a good man. Regardless of anything that Frank, or anyone else, ever said or did to me, there is one thing I'm very sure of. I'm a National Championship head coach of arguably the best team in the history of Minor League football, and that is good enough for me.

# Addressing the Issue of Abuse

*Remember No One Can Make You Feel Inferior Without Your Consent*
  *-Eleanor Roosevelt*

I was a child with an abusive adult in my life. I have the greatest respect for anyone out there raising children. I know the challenges that parents face trying to provide a good place for kids to grow. Between work, our commitments, and the unpredictability of life, we encounter challenges and tension that can affect the home. Whatever you do, do not let the challenges and tensions in your life lead to abusing others – especially your children and those closest to you. If you or anyone you know is dealing with anger issues or you are on the brink of hitting a child, spouse, girlfriend, or anyone else, I hope my story makes you pause and seek the help you need.

Once you start abusing someone, whether verbally, mentally, or physically, it takes a toll—on you and your victim. I am begging you to not do it because you will change people's lives forever. I was fortunate that my mom instilled in me a strong desire to succeed in spite of my circumstances. Other victims are not as lucky. The collateral damage in a victim's life can be so great that they never recover.

If you are confronted by or become aware of a bully at school or online, please notify the principals, teachers, or anyone and offer help as quickly as possible. Your help could change a life and most importantly in many cases you may end up saving a life.

If you are dealing with abuse, please know that you are loved and that you can make it through. I know at times it seems there is no-where to turn—that no one can help you. But there are hotlines with great people who will help you if you make the call. I hope you find solace in my story, I hope you find strength in my story and I hope that in some way big or small that I may inspire you to never give up, because you are a great person with a future that is without lim-its. Don't let anyone ever tell you anything different.

### Hotlines

| | |
|---|---|
| In immediate risk or harm? | Call 911 |
| Childhelp National Child Abuse Hotline | 1-800-4-A-CHILD (1-800-422-4453) |
| National Coalition Against Do-mestic Violence Domestic Abuse Hotline | 1-800-799-7233 |
| National Suicide Prevention Life-line | 1-800-273-TALK (8255) |

### Other Resources

| | |
|---|---|
| Alcoholics Anonymous | www.aa.org |
| Narcotics Anonymous | www.na.org |
| Al-Anon: helping families of alcoholics | www.al-anon.org |
| NAR-ANON: helping families of addicts | www.nar-anon.org |

## About the Author

Jamie King is a 25 year broadcast veteran of radio and television. He hosted the Mark Rypien Show on the Home Team Sports (currently Comcast SportsNet) with former Super Bowl MVP Quarterback Mark Rypien of the Washington Redskins. He has appeared in segments on the USA Network as well as FOX Television in Washington, D.C.. He has hosted numerous radio shows as well and is currently the host of the "Sports King" radio program which airs simultaneously on ESPN Radio on 950AM throughout Central Virginia. King has interviewed some of sports all time greatest athletes including Wayne Gretzky, Bo Jackson, Michael Jordan and Cal Ripken Jr.. King was the Head Coach of the Minor League Football team (The Fredericksburg Generals) leading them to a National Championship in 1996 while posting a 13-0 record. King recruited and Coached the 1982 NFL-MVP former Washington Redskins Kicker Mark Moseley to play for the National Championship Generals. He was voted as the National Coach of The Year for the American Football Association in 1996 and was inducted into the Mason Dixon Football Leagues Hall of Fame in 1998.

Have a Story to Tell?

Need help figuring out how to get it written?

Need help getting it published?

We helped Jamie to create the book he wanted, and we can help you, too!

To find out how, visit http://www.bigcloudmedia.com/story

Made in the USA
Lexington, KY
04 May 2017